About the Author

Lisa Lampanelli skyrocketed to comedy fame thanks to her jaw-dropping performances on the Comedy Central roasts of Jeff Foxworthy, Pamela Anderson, William Shatner, and Flavor Flav, among others. A regular on *The Tonight Show* and *The Howard Stern Show*, Lisa continues to sell out the theaters across the country with her sweetly served but acerbic stand-up wit. Her CD/DVD *Dirty Girl* was nominated for a Grammy for Best Comedy Album in 2007 and her first HBO special, *Long Live the Queen*, premiered to spectacular numbers in 2009. This fall, she will shoot a one-hour stand-up special for Comedy Central, scheduled for release in early 2011.

Advance Praise for Lisa Lampanelli and
Chocolate, Please

"L.L. Lana Lang, Lois Lane, Lex Luthor, and now the greatest of them all, Lisa Lampanelli. She is funny. She's the one person who will be invited to a roast and destroy everything in her path and leave you wondering who could follow her. Lisa will steal the show every time, whether it's on my radio program or on any stage anywhere doing stand-up. And don't forget, she has those iconic initials that all great people have in Superman comics: L.L. I love Lisa and so should you. A true original and a brilliant comedy mind."

—HOWARD STERN

"If you want to see real racial integration, go to a Lisa Lampanelli show. That's where you'll find people of every color and creed having a good laugh at themselves and each other. No one is safe from prejudice at a Lisa Lampanelli show . . . and no one wants to be. By boldly poking fun at everyone, including her chocolate-daddy-lovin' self, Lisa releases us from a prison of cultural guilt. She's more than a stand-up. She's a standout."

—JIM CARREY

"Lisa is awesome. I've known Lisa from way back when she was a thin Chinese woman. I love Lisa. Not only is she offstage one of the sweetest girls I've ever met, but onstage she turns into Don Rickles only with more hair and not as shapely. And nobody gets bigger laughs than Lisa. Lisa is bringing to theaters across the country something Americans seem to have lost—a sense of humor and the ability to laugh at themselves. Lisa accomplishes both those tasks when she's onstage. She's an unbelievably great comedian. What she does is not easy in the environment we live in today.

And Lisa pulls it off. She's a true pro. I will say this though: I'm about half sick and tired of that bitch weaselin' her way into all my movies! The hell with Lisa and this book! Buy mine!!!!"

—LARRY THE CABLE GUY

"Lisa can tie me down to a bed anytime."

—LL COOL J

"Lisa is the most outrageous comic we have ever had on *The Tonight Show*."

—JAY LENO

"Jesus—this book is filthy."

—SARAH SILVERMAN

"Every generation has a female comic that destroys the conventional wisdom that only men can be raunchy and funny. Lisa Lampanelli is this generation's choice."

—CARLOS MENCIA

Chocolate, Please

Lisa Lampanelli

Chocolate, Please

My Adventures in Food, Fat, and Freaks

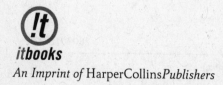

!t
itbooks
An Imprint of HarperCollins*Publishers*

itbooks

This is a work of nonfiction. The events and experiences detailed herein are all true and have been faithfully rendered as I have remembered them, to the best of my ability. Some names, identities, and circumstances have been changed in order to protect the integrity and/or anonymity of the various individuals involved. Though conversations come from my keen recollection of them, they are not written to represent word-for-word documentation; rather, I've retold them in a way that evokes the real feeling and meaning of what was said, in keeping with the true essence of the mood and spirit of the event.

A hardcover edition of this book was published in 2009 by It Books, an imprint of HarperCollins Publishers.

HarperCollins books may be purchased for educational, business, or sales promotional use. For information please write: Special Markets Department, HarperCollins Publishers, 10 East 53rd Street, New York, NY 10022.

First It Books paperback published 2010.

The Library of Congress has catalogued the hardcover edition as follows:

Lampanelli, Lisa.
    Chocolate, please : my adventures in food, fat, and freaks / Lisa Lampanelli.—1st ed.
      p. cm.
    ISBN 978-0-06-173315-4
    1. Lampanelli, Lisa. 2. Women comedians—United States—Biography. I. Title.
    PN2287.L244A3 2009
    792.7'6028092—dc22

                                 2009012223

ISBN 978-0-06-173316-1 (pbk.)

10 11 12 13 14 OV/RRD 10 9 8 7 6 5 4 3 2 1

I would like to dedicate this book to the two people who have shaped my life and made me the person I am today. No, not world-famous mimes Shields and Yarnell. My parents, Leonard and Gloria. You are my true soul mates.

Contents

· · · · · · · · · · · · ·

part one

What I'm Known For

CHAPTER ONE

Once You Go Black...

It was Valentine's Day 2000—and I wasn't exactly in the best place I've ever been. I was eighty pounds overweight, I was working the weekend at Pips Comedy Club in Brooklyn, and I was miserable.

You don't understand—this was really weird for me 'cause believe it or not, I have always been the chick who *loves* Valentine's Day. I know what you're thinking: "What? Lisa Lampanelli, the Queen of Mean, the insult comic, the chick who is to romance what Rosie O'Donnell is to beauty pageants—

Lisa Lampanelli loves Valentine's Day?" Yes, fuckers, I love Valentine's Day. Deal with it!

I love the little inedible candy hearts with the stupid messages, I love the tiny paper cards with the white envelopes where the glue never works, I love the cheesy flower arrangements held together by that big green piece of Styrofoam. I never had any reason to hate Valentine's Day. Hey, what wasn't to love? Every year since I was twelve, I had a boyfriend. Today, people might call that codependent. Back then, the word hadn't even been invented yet! I just thought I was popular!

Now, when you have a boyfriend for every single Valentine's Day for more than twenty-five years, you get pretty used to it. But Valentine's Day 2000 was different. That was my first Valentine's Day alone. By choice. And—I'll be honest with ya—it stunk!

So, why would a single woman just shy of forty suddenly decide to be alone? Three words: Dr. Joy Browne. Dr. Joy is my favorite radio shrink and I'd been listening to her for about a year. She is convinced people should take a year off between relationships to see what they really want—and *who* they really want to be with. So, after my last breakup that November, I decided to give her theory a try. Hey, she's a Jewish shrink with her own national radio show and a great relationship of her own, and she wrote *Dating for Dummies*. How could this bitch be wrong?

Lemme go back a little. See, I always had boyfriends, sure. But they were never guys I wanted to brag about. They were never the catch, the prize. They were never guys my girlfriends tried to steal when I was in the bathroom. I woulda killed for that!

That's because I always went after guys I knew I could get. But they were never guys who really got *me*. There was just this long string of near-misses: the junior varsity long jumper in high school, the electrical engineering major in college, the bass player. Those guys never got me all three ways—get your mind outta the gutter, people, *not* all three inputs! I mean mind, body, and soul. And they turned out to be about as hot as Jared from Subway.

Oh, come on—don't even front! Like none o' you has ever settled for someone beneath you? Everyone has! Drew Barrymore has long since done better than Tom Green. And J. Lo has moved on from Cris Judd! Like that had a fucking prayer! I can't believe Courteney Cox is still married to that 1-800-retard.

That being said, I would have killed to date any one of those a-holes. See, all my life, it's been the same. Chubby and white. I married a chubby white guy, I replaced him with a chubby white guy, and I inserted another chubby white guy here, which, by the way, is what the tattoo on my inner thigh says.

Jimmy Pantelones was my first chubby white guy—and I thought I was *the shit*! I was in the eighth grade and I had a boyfriend, one who liked what I liked—Jethro Tull, makin' out, and cake. Especially cake! And it didn't matter that he was shorter than me, had an out-of-control mass of wiry black hair, and resembled Howard Stern's Baba Booey. I had music, food, and affection. Who was better than me? No one!!

Twenty years and forty-two chubby white guys later, it was no better.

There was Frank. People called him Big Frank—and

rightfully so. Frank went about four hundred pounds. Four hundred pounds! Lemme illustrate that for you people who don't go to the circus—you know how your guy's underwear says BVD? His says "Boulevard." Frank was so big, he used Twinkies for suppositories. Frank was so big that as soon as he stepped in the ocean, it was high tide.

Aw, c'mon—I joke. Frank *was* big. But it didn't matter. He was *suave*!

It's true! Frank oozed Soprano charm. Every date with him was like that scene from *Goodfellas*. You know, the one where Ray Liotta tips everyone in the kitchen? Only with us, Frank wasn't tipping. He was paying for the dishes he knocked over with his love handles.

Frank would give me anything I wanted. "Hey, Lisa—*any-thing*—you say it, it's *done*! Ya know, I'm connected." Connected! What a turn-on!

Frank wasn't lyin'; he *was* connected—to a fork! It only took me four months of dating him to figure out that Frank wasn't a gangster—he was just *fat*! Frank wasn't in the mob—Frank *was* a mob.

Frank really wasn't that bad. He was actually the best of the worst. I've been dating forever and my list of exes reads like the inhabitants of the Island of Misfit Boys: Big Frank, Stalker Pete, Retard Jim. Looking back now, I can see that I always dated the undatable.

There was Needy Steve. Steve was five foot three and Jewish. *And* he had hair plugs. What the fuck was I thinking? But worse, he was clingy!

"I'm sorry, I'm sorry. I hope I'm not overstepping. I-I-I-I know we've only known each other for a week, but I hope you will accept this key to my apartment, my humble abode. That way you can cook for me and I can have a nice meal to come home to. Doesn't that sound good, Mommy?"

Mommy! Ewww! He wanted me to be his *mother*! Hey, I'll breastfeed him. But cooking! *No!!*

Ross the Half-a-Fag—holy crap! All I can say about him is: "Hey, Lisa, guess what!! I'm not gay anymore." Not gay any-more!! "*No!!!* I swear, I'm not. That was a long time ago." Now I'm not saying gay guys aren't terrific—in fact, if it wasn't for gay guys, us fat chicks would have no friends. Just don't try to make out with one of them—it hurts! "Hey, homo, it's a nipple—not a dick. Ease up!"

Funeral Frank! Now, don't get all depressed—don't worry. Funeral Frank isn't dead. I call him Funeral Frank because I picked him up at my uncle's funeral.

Walking slowly down the receiving line of mourners, I par-roted the phrase I'd heard at every funeral I'd ever attended: "I'm sorry for your loss. I'm sorry for your loss." But just then a hot leather daddy walked into the funeral parlor and caught my eye. Wow! He was hot. His name was Frank, he was an old family friend—and he looked like a biker! Rrrrrrrr!!

After careful investigation, I found out Funeral Frank drove a Harley and worked for the phone company! Wow, benefits!

I was out of control! My uncle was about to get planted, and I was lookin' to get plowed! It was shameless! I might as well have said to the funeral director, "Hey, you got any room in the back of that hearse? Move the coffin over—it's gonna be a long night."

I had to get this under control. Looking back, I realize these guys were nothing more than space fillers—I thought they'd help fill in where my self-esteem left off. But since the guys I picked weren't exactly grade-A meat, there was still space left. And since I was lonely even *with* the guys in my life, I filled that extra space with food.

✿

So, back to Valentine's Day. I was alone and my weight was at an all-time high. To make my punishment complete, I was working the weekend at—did I mention?—Pips. Pips! Pips was comedy hell—a club in Sheepshead Bay, Brooklyn, whose only claim to fame was that it spawned Andrew Dice Clay. And they were *proud* of it! So there I was, at the goombah capital of the world, and since it was Valentine's Day, *everyone* was paired off. I mean *everyone*!!! Imagine date night at the Bada Bing—only not as classy.

So I started scopin' around for single guys. Hey, fat I could handle. Alone I could handle. Fat *and* alone—fuck that! Take your year off and shove it up your twat, Dr. Joy! (By the way, I think it's this line that kept Dr. Joy from writing the foreword to this book.)

I looked around and spotted one guy alone at the end of the bar. And you can just imagine what a hunk o' burnin' love this one was. Screw it—I was by myself. I needed it! I was goin' in!

"You're Sal? Nice to meet you. Oh, you drive a city bus . . . What route? Oh, the 102. Excellent." Somebody kill me, please!

Not even one minute of awkward flirting later, the door to the club opened and in walked this little person, this midget. And you know what? I was impressed. I had to give this bitch credit. She came in *alone*—I was only there alone because I was working. And—you ain't gonna believe this—before I knew what was happening, this lollipop broad walked right up to Sal, *my* Sal, and get this, Ralph Kramden lifted her up onto a barstool and they started talking. So there I was— watching this she-elf cockblock me. And you know what? Everybody has their wall and it was at that moment that I hit mine. I figured out what had just happened: Sal chose the midget over me!

The great thing about hitting the wall is you can finally see things clearly. This chick was my hero. She had more self-esteem than me and she was half my size! I couldn't believe it—I was actually looking *up* to a dwarf.

I'm not saying it didn't hurt. I mean, at first, I got defensive. I wanted to rant that it's a *sad fuckin' day* when a normal-sized guy would rather bang a midget than Lisa Lampanelli, *Comedy's Lovable Queen of Mean, headliner at Carolines on Broadway*! But you know what? It was cool that she walked in by herself *and* it was cool that Sal—this bus-driving chooch from Brooklyn—had the guts to pick her. But there was one thing I couldn't figure out: Besides the one-in-a-million chance she came with a pot of gold, what did she have that I didn't have?

Driving home that night, I was feeling sorry for myself. I had to change the way I was living, but what was I supposed to do? I never wanted Sal in the first place, so why did I even go after him? That got me thinking. What would it be like to go after one that I wanted? I'd never done that. Ever since freshman year of high school when Ronnie Campanaro chose Lori Pagliarulo over me, I shot low. But what do I want? What do I want? I'll admit that at that moment, I wanted cheese! Hot cheese! Dripping hot melting cheese! Who moved my cheese? One door closes, a window opens. Everything happens for a reason. If it's meant to be, it's meant to be . . . And suddenly the most profound thought hit me:

No more cheesy guys ever!

Hey, I know it's not as clever as one of Dr. Phil's sayings, but I knew one thing—I'd rather be alone than bottom-feed ever again!

❁

I drove home with all those Oprah-isms flying around my head and they finally started to sink in. True, I got home and flopped down in front of the TV with a bag of peanut M&M's. Shut up—I'm supposed to change everything in one night?!?! And I got the remote. Somehow I stumbled on the MTV Video Music Awards just as Jagged Edge, four R&B guys I'd never heard of, were onstage with the hottest rapper that year—Nelly.

Despite or maybe partly because of my Valentine's "Rejection and Sugar" cocktail, I couldn't help but notice that Nelly was hot in more ways than one. Nelly had muscles. Nelly had a stocking-thingie on his head and a Band-Aid on his mocha-colored cheek. "I bet he fights a lot," I thought. "Hmmm . . ."

Laying in bed alone, watching, I started feeling a little— y'know—different, like I got a little tug. Hey, this guy was cute—*no*, he wasn't cute; screw cute! Jared from Subway was "cute." This guy on TV was tough, he was rough, he was *naughty*. He was dangerous, he was sweaty, and I was getting really *hot.* So, that's how people feel when they say they're "turned on"!

I should mention that this was new for me. I mean, yeah, I'd done the nasty before—*if you could call it that.* Sex wasn't fun or fulfilling—it was something I did to keep a boyfriend. So, watching Nelly, I was like, "What the fuck is goin' on here?" I had to compose myself!! I was the fat chick, the funny chick, the tough chick, not the sexy chick. Girls like me weren't supposed to get hot and bothered over gangsta rappers!

But oh my God! There he was rapping about "If you wanna go and take a ride with me" and Jagged Edge asking, "Where da party at?" and that little thug Ja Rule serenading J. Lo wearing nothin' but leather pants, long platinum chains, and a scowl! Who *were* these guys and where had they been hiding?

Turns out they hadn't been hiding; I had. Well, what do you want? I grew up in Connecticut. The Connecticut license plate should say, "Connecticut: You won't find your clitoris here!" In Connecticut, you follow the rules: You meet a guy in college and you marry that guy and that guy may not be perfect, but he sure as shit is white—except maybe in Bridgeport. It's not like I was living in a bubble! I had *seen* black guys before—they had always been there. But back in Connecticut, they didn't go with my pearls and sweater sets.

But watching TV that night, I started remembering stuff of a darker nature—these deeply buried images just popped up. Images of hot black guys with fat white chicks on daytime talk shows. Or the time I was shopping at Ashley Stewart—the store for fat black chicks—and saw these hot black security guards flirting with *fat* women! And the women were loving it! How many shows had I done with hunky black guys in the audience sitting with women who had huge tits, huge asses, and even huger self-esteem?

What *is* it about black men and fat women? These sexy, handsome, and—let's not forget—manly men digging a big woman? They even talk about it in their music! Black guys sing baby's got "back"—black slang for a big ass—and they mean it as a compliment! They don't even say fat. They call it "thick" and they *pursue* it! In fact, when they insult a woman, *that's* when they use the word "skinny." "Look at that thin-lipped bony-assed bitch!" So why had I never considered black guys?

Then a vivid memory hit me. It was about ten years before, when I was walking near the Port Authority Bus Terminal and I heard the voice of this brother calling after me: "Honey, I just got three words for you: mmmm, mmmm, mmmm!" Even though I blushed, I thought I was the *shit* for hours after that. And finally I remembered hurrying out of a heavy metal club in my twenties, head held low after being rejected by another roomful of white guys, and the black cab driver saying, "No one should have a bad day, baby! *No one!* Especially not a fine piece o' womanhood as yourself."

Womanhood! I couldn't even *imagine* a white guy *saying* "womanhood"! The white guys I knew didn't even notice I *had* womanhood or know what the fuck womanhood was. And the cab driver was right—I *didn't* deserve to have a bad day. I *was* a fine piece of womanhood. And I started to get it, that thing that Sal and the midget had: They accepted themselves, they were comfortable with themselves, and that was attractive, that was *sexy*—and it was real.

So after seeing the MTV awards and watching BET for two months like it was the Religion Channel, my head was spinning like that little bitch's in *The Exorcist*. It was as if some big Rubik's Cube in my head clicked into place. All the colors on the cube finally lined up and on *all six sides, the color was black*!!

❖

Three weeks later, I woke up in a black guy's bed. Hey, when I decide to make a change, I work fast.

It happened one night when I was performing at the Comic Strip in New York—and *my pants fit*!

That's right—they fit, motherfucker! It's that simple. Not profound enough for ya? Maybe you expected me to reveal some painful secret I discovered doing the *Life Strategies* workbook with Dr. Phil, but hey, you want the truth, right? And the truth is my pants fit and that rocked. Pants from 1985! Sure, they were out of style, stonewashed, and completely faggy, something that Belinda Carlisle would have worn on a fat day, but they were my pants and they were hanging right. I had lost twenty pounds! Yes, I still had sixty more to go, but that night I felt—I can't even believe I am saying this—I felt "sexy."

So I was at the Comic Strip and it was one of those nights when there were like ten people in the audience. From the stage, I could see every single two-drink-minimum motherfucker in the audience, and trust me, they could definitely see me—I'm big and loud and not easily ignored. So I was on-stage and I spotted this one guy right at the front table. There he was, the guy I always get—that nice, boring white guy, slightly overweight, less overweight if you squint. The kind of guy I've been dating since I was twelve. The kind of guy who probably has a good heart and a good job and always has just enough clueless self-esteem to talk to me after every single show. "There he is," I thought, "there's Lisa's next boyfriend."

In the middle of my next joke, my eyes wandered to the back of the room, way back, and I saw a guy—let's just call him Big Daddy. Big Daddy was every naughty black taboo rolled into one—do-rag, baggy pants, tank top showing muscles, dark sunglasses. I couldn't even guess what a guy like this did for a living. He looked like a drug dealer who worked as a security guard at Staples on the side.

I was faced with a choice. Right in front of me was vanilla. Way in the back was chocolate. In that moment, I made a decision: "I want chocolate!"

I decided to feel Big Daddy out. I started joking around with him from the stage, saying things like, "You know you want it, beeyotch!" and pointing to my ass and saying, "C'mon, baby, I'll give you something to hide behind when the cops start shooting." And he looked like he was *into it*. Not "Man, she's a funny bitch" into it, but "I'll take you up on your offer" into it. I stuck my hand in my pocket and felt the bagginess of my jeans for courage. Oh, yeah, I may have had sixty pounds to lose, but that night I was skinny! I was smokin'. I was Madonna in that "Borderline" video and Tawny Kitaen crawling around on the hood of Whitesnake's car. I was gonna go for it! I was gonna have that brownie sundae and swallow every bite.

A few minutes later, after my set, I was standing at the bar of the Comic Strip. Lemme tell you, comics who stand at the bar after their sets are either drunks or trying to get laid, and put it this way: I don't drink. So here I was waiting, trying to look like this was just another fabulously fun night at the club—haha har-dee-har-har—trying not to play with my hair. And who comes right at me—the vanilla pound cake, the white-bread bologna sandwich I could pick up in my sleep. And of course I got sucked into a conversation.

"Thanks, I'm glad you liked it. Good . . . uh-huh, yeah, it's great . . . Upper West Side—uh-huh . . . Originally? Trumbull, Connecticut." Jesus Christ, *where the hell is the black one*??? "Your sister's up there too. Great, great. Oh, these? The Gap." God, I *hate* the white devil!

Then I saw him. There he was—Big Daddy! Coming right through the doorway! And the conversation I was having with Mayonnaise turned to white noise. All I saw was Big Daddy, and he was looking my way. Our eyes met and then he started looking at the headshots on the wall. Oh, c'mon, that brother *did not* care about those pictures, and I seriously didn't care where this white a-hole's sister lived. Big Daddy was waiting to talk to me—I could *feel* it. But there was Flounder from *Animal House* jawin' away: "So uh, how did you ever get up the nerve to try comedy?"

"Actually, I am trying to work up the nerve to make a move on Snoop Dogg over there, but you won't shut the fuck up!" I thought. Lisa! Come on, Lisa! Get yourself together. Remember what Oprah said about the Power of Now! *Now!* Let your pants do the walking and your ass do the talking! I said, "Excuse me, I gotta go." And with that, Baggy Pants Lampanelli was dust in the wind.

I sidled up behind Big Daddy. "You know you ain't lookin' at those pictures, dawg." Dawg! Who the fuck was I? P. Diddy?

"You know you're just trying to work up the nerve to talk to me. Well, I am the queen."

"And I'll be your king."

King!!! RRRRR! This was *good*! Twenty pounds ago, I would have looked around to see if he was talking to some other white bitch. But that night, I didn't.

"You'll be my king? Oh, really, is that right?"

"That's right—when can I see you again?"

Cripes, that was easy. Were all black men like this? Two sentences in, and I had practically sealed the deal.

I played my whole hand: "That depends—do you mean see my comedy or see me? If you want to see me, I'll give you my number, but if you mean see my comedy, call the club."

"No, it's all you, girl."

Oh my God—he was talking "black" to me. I felt like I was in an Usher video.

I gave him my number and tried to look cool as I walked outside. Then I raced to my car. My face was flushed, my armpits were sweatin'. I hardly got my foot in the door before I slammed it. I grabbed my cell phone and dialed: "Oh, my God!!! I just hit on my first black!! . . . I don't know, I might not even bang him! . . . Yes, I'll let you know . . . Yes, *if* I bang him, I'll tell you if they're circumcised . . . Mom." I'm kidding—it was my dad. All right, it was my friend Ro. This was the first time I could ever remember a girlfriend of mine actually being interested in my sex life! This was fun. Lisa Lampanelli was having fun for once in her life. About fucking time. Who knew losing weight, going to the shrink, and doing the work to get my shit together would be *fun*! Thank you, Dr. Phil, Oprah, and Dr. Joy—thank you the Bald, the Black, and the Jew! I finally had the balls to flirt with a decent piece of ass! A piece of ass who wanted to date me!

Or so I thought . . .

❀

The day of our first date, my cell phone rang at four P.M. "Hey, baby." Oh, isn't that sweet? He's calling to say he can't wait to see me later. "Listen, today ain't gonna happen."

"*What?!*"

"My cousin got into some trouble and I have to post his bail."

Bail? Oh, c'mon. I knew he was black, but there's no way he was falling into a stereotype this soon. Those blacks! I am never talking to him again. I didn't say a word.

"I hope you ain't mad at me, boo."

"Of course I'm mad at you! I hate you! Your cousin's more important to you than me!"

"Well, he's not really my cousin—I know him since I'm five years old. We just come up together."

"I don't care! I wish you both were dead!" Who the hell did I think I was? Scarlett O'Hara saying "fiddle-di-di"?

People, don't worry. I do realize how ridiculous this sounds now. I know I sound like a complete mental patient, but I was *freaking!* Every black stereotype I'd heard over the years was rattling around in my head: "Great! Is this what I'm in for? Men who cancel dates because they're posting bond and going to child-support hearings? Oh, my God, if I commit to the Dark Side, am I committing myself to a life straight out of Ricki Lake?"

"C'mon, baby—I can't help it . . . I'm just reliable. You'd

think you would like the type of brother who his friends can look to."

He was right. He *was* reliable. Wow!

We rescheduled.

Exactly a week later, the phone rang. It was nine o'clock at night. "Hey, baby."

"Where *are* you?"

"Now, don't be mad, baby. Why you got to be like that? I had some trouble with my kids." Kids!!!!

"You have kids?"

"Yeah, I told you." He told me? Oh, really, when? When had he told me he had kids? On our first date? No—'cause we *hadn't had* a first date. I wanted to rip his heart out of his chest. And then I thought about that chest!

Finally, I started to get the picture. We hadn't had a first date because we would *never* have a first date. Andre—that's Big Daddy's real name—was never going to be my boyfriend. What was I doing? This guy had kids, he'd canceled twice, and posting bail was normal to him. It had taken me two weeks of living in denial but I started to have some perspective. This guy was *undatable*!!!

Undatable, yes, but, goddamn it, he wasn't unfuckable.

Hey, if guys could think with their dicks, so could I!

CHAPTER TWO

Chocolate, Please

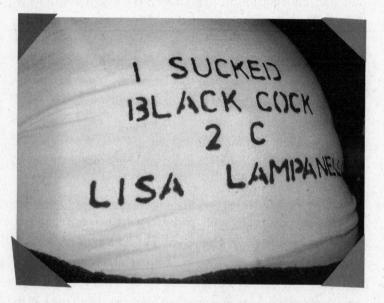

wenty minutes later, I walked into Andre's apartment building with only one thing on my mind. We had agreed that he would take a shower and I would come up to his apartment and meet him for "a drink." I, in the meantime, got dressed for sex—I even wore high heels! I hadn't been on a date in a while but I was pretty sure guys still liked high heels. I buttoned my coat right up to the top so the Spanish kids on the block wouldn't goof on me for being in their neighborhood just to bang a brother—even though they definitely would have been right!

I walked into Andre's apartment building and, oh, great! He was on the fourth floor—*with no elevator!* There was no doubt I was gonna break a freakin' sweat. I didn't work out! I was just starting to get in shape. My feet were killing me, and my control-top pantyhose were bagging up in the crotch. To make matters worse, my high heels were making all this noise on the stairs! God—I had to make it upstairs undiscovered. I pictured Andre anticipating my arrival from my thundering steps, me panting, sweating, wheezing, groping the handrail like an old lady. Oh, yeah, that would be sexy! Yeah, nothing turns a man on like a fat lady sweating! No, I had to be quiet, graceful. I needed to make it up the stairs with time to spare to get myself together and maintain the illusion that I was fly.

I don't know how I did it, but I got to the top without being discovered. I took a minute to catch my breath, regroup. I stepped over a girl's pink bicycle and knocked.

"Hi, baby. You look beautiful. Let me take your coat." Oh, my God! This mother-f-er was *built!* I unbuttoned the trench coat, handed it to him, and watched him walk down the hall to hang it up. I quickly checked out the apartment—my mother always told me to do that in case I had to make a quick escape, like if a guy is getting too frisky and you feel he's gonna rape you. Then I remembered—that's why I was there.

"Sit down—do you want some wine?"

"Sure!" Andre poured me a glass. I hate wine and I hadn't had a drink in years, but I needed courage. If I slept with him, I was gonna have to wiggle out of my control-top pantyhose in a half-sexy way, so I figured I better have some wine. After I had a few glasses of wine, I could fart and think it was sexy.

I sat on the couch—it was either that or the floor. "I'm gonna buy some furniture soon when I have the money," Andre explained. "My wife took everything but I ain't mad. I'm just tryin' to be a brother that improves himself." That was so great! We had a lot in common already—he was into self-help too. Wait a minute—what was I thinking? No furniture, no money, wife! I made up my mind to fuck this guy and run.

"You look really sexy, girl," Andre said to me from the kitchen, where he was standing, sipping—I shit you not—an Olde English forty out of the bottle. I was eye-level with the top of his sweatpants. I saw proof that he *definitely* thought I was sexy. And just as I was trying to put together a lame "Is that a plantain in your pocket or are you happy to see me?" joke to break the tension, Andre sat right down next to me with his face only an inch from mine! I smelled the malt liquor on his breath (thirty black guys later, that smell still gets me hot!). I felt tipsier and tipsier—almost buzzed enough to drown out the doubts in my head: "Oh, my God, I *can't* sleep with him. I don't *love* him. Isn't sex supposed to be about love?"

Just then, the wine started talking to me: "What are you talking about? He's separated! Besides, look at you. You're sitting on a Levitz couch and looking at a velvet Nefertiti wall hanging. He has three kids and he drinks forties *out of the bottle!* His sheets are leopard print and he has a view of a brick wall. Lisa, let's be honest—you don't have to worry about getting too attached or, as Dr. Joy would say, 'enmeshed' in a relationship with this!"

By the way, everything I'm telling you is the God's honest truth here. You might think it's way too stereotypical, but it's *all* true. I mean it! You can see for yourself—I'll give you

Andre's phone number. Call him! Trust me—it'll be disconnected.

Still, I was terrified at what might happen next. Suppose
"it" was too big, suppose he wanted to—*do it different.* I heard
black guys loved that. Suppose it *looked* weird? I heard black
guys' dicks are purple. "No, no, I shouldn't," I thought. And as
soon as I thought "shouldn't," everything fell into place. That's
when I heard my shrink's voice. Dr. Judy always said, "Don't
do what you *should* do. Do what you *want* to do!"

Well, I knew what I wanted. Screw the kids, screw the
imitation-leather sofa, and screw those doubts. I knew what
I wanted—I wanted out of those pantyhose and into that
motherfucker's pants.

❖

You know, years ago, I worked in publishing. One of my first
jobs was at *Us* magazine, a magazine full of "beautiful people."
Beautiful! Ha! *I* was a real beaut myself. I was a twenty-five-
year-old, size-twenty-four fact-checker. I had a two-hour
commute and a diploma from a summer course at Harvard—
and I worked at Us *magazine!* You'd think the Harvard shit
would've at least gotten me into *People!*

A lot of the female editors decorated their offices like they
were on staff at *Tiger Beat.* Johnny Depp, Bono, Rob Lowe—
all over the place. But not me! I prided myself on *not* liking hot
guys. "Those shallow bitches," I'd say to myself as I proofed
a story on Judd Nelson's favorite ice cream. "I *hate* good-
looking guys. I like guys with substance, guys like Anthony
Michael Hall!"

In reality, though, let's be honest. I didn't hate *hot* guys.

My problem was I never felt like I could *get* hot guys. Instead I hung up pictures of Jethro Tull, Simply Red, and Gerard Depardieu, and dated their unfamous equivalents.

Well, fifteen years and one hot guy later, guess what, folks? I didn't hate hot guys—I *loved* 'em! And I started going after them. Andre had gotten me hooked! They were new to me. Finally I could walk down the street with a guy and have other girls say, "Where'd you get *that* one!" That had *never* happened to me before. I know it might sound shallow, but for once in my life, I didn't want the smart one, I didn't want the funny one, I wanted the *hot* one. Andre was my first piece of fine chocolate—and I started going through men like New York City was a Godiva wholesaler. And to be honest, my mouth was always full!

By the way, this is the point in every story where the woman says, "But don't worry, I wasn't a whore." Well, guess what, folks? I wasn't a whore either! Yeah, I hooked up with a lot of black men. Some I slept with, some I just teased. Most of them were flings, some I dated for "respectable" lengths of time. I even hit on other guys when my dude was in the bathroom. Sometimes I called them after sex, sometimes I didn't. And I *never* returned calls after lousy sex. I wasn't a whore, people. I was a "guy."

That was me! Six months in "guy mode." I checked men out, I hit on them when they pulled up in their cars, and my favorite thing to do—it still makes me laugh—was to look a black guy up and down on the street and say, "Now, *that's* what I'm talking about." I learned how to flirt, how to stick out my ass, walk to the end of the bar, look around, and flip my hair—*all* at the same time—and I don't wanna brag, but I hooked an average of about one in three. That's pretty good! I wasn't nervous anymore—that feeling was long gone—and now I just wanted to have fun. I had some lost time to make up for! I got rid of the voice that said, "Oh, Lisa, two men in two days! What *are* you thinking?" Thinking? I wasn't thinking. I just bagged 'em, tagged 'em, gave myself a high five, and slapped myself on the ass.

To my credit, I'm very goal oriented. I decided that I should approach dating like it was my job. I figured salesmen had to meet quotas and so did I. If I didn't hit on at least three men a night, I hadn't made my numbers and I would have to compensate for it the next night.

But, like Oprah and Suze Orman say, life isn't just about acquiring wealth—it's about giving 10 percent back. So, ladies, here's my 10 percent. This is directed at any of you white women out there who want to go to the Dark Continent, who are thinking of paying a visit to the Ivory Coast.

Here it is: *Everything you've heard about black men is true.* That's right—after six months on my chocolate diet, I knew every stereotype in the book. Black men have baby mama drama, they don't tip, they don't have long-distance phone service, and they certainly juggle more than one woman at a time. They hustle, they drink Belvedere and Alizé, they lie and look hot doing it. They yell at the movie screen, steal at work, and complain that the man is holding them down. *But there's some stuff you never hear about black men that's also true.* Black men will open the car door for you, black men write poetry and love to cuddle, and they pay their child support and practically wallpaper their houses with pictures of their kids, who they miss terribly. Oh, yeah, and there's another stereotype that's also true. Black men give you the most passionate sex of your life, you will love that when you hold hands it looks like a Benetton ad, and you will be called the next day—in fact, in most cases, *that same night*—when a black man takes your number. Most important to me, though, they will never, ever be in an argument with you and say, "Oh, yeah? Well, you're fat!"

Instead they say magic words like "Don't lose that ass, girl!" and they say it so sincerely and deeply that you don't mind that they might be saying it to three other women that same night. You feel beautiful, and for that moment, it's all good.

Every stereotype is true and none of the stereotypes is true. It's all about the man.

How'd I learn all this? For the entire year after Andre, as I lost more than sixty pounds, I ran an Underground Railroad through my apartment. It was raining black men on a daily basis, and I had learned to have fun! I felt appreciated, and my size 24s shrank to 16s. My train had pulled into Brown Town, and I wasn't leaving the station any time soon!

And as my waist shrank, my Booty Call Book bulged.

Let's see—there were my size-22 guys. Andre, who you know; and Moose.

Moose was a heartbreaker. Twenty-four years old, two kids, great dancer. He talked to me like I was a duchess: "It is my honor to be with you." But he lied a lot and stood me up. I could get that when I was *really* fat. I moved on.

My size-20 men were Ben and Patch. When I asked Ben what he did for a living, he said, "I'm a hustler, baby." He was. He turned up at my house, lit up a joint, and showed me a bag with a velour sweat suit and jewelry he'd bought for $100. I didn't care what he smoked or what he did. I did *him*.

Patch had one eye, three bullet wounds, and lots of martial arts injuries. Black guys *love* the martial arts. Patch told me within one hour that he loved me—and I believed it for the next twenty-four. Until I never heard from him again.

Wayne came along when I hit size 18. With fifty pounds down, I figured I'd upgrade to guys with solid professions. Wayne was a cop. But, one problem—he was married. By size 18, even *I* knew that married is no good. Ten pounds earlier, I might have seen him again, but now that I had good highlights and smaller clothes, I wouldn't arrest him.

Kenny was a male stripper—hey, I said my size-18 guys had solid professions, not noble ones. Kenny was a freak—he wore leather everywhere, every day, even at the barber shop in 98-degree heat. What a moron! But what a body! I couldn't stop staring at his muscles. Christ—don't even bang me, just leave a picture. Holler!

I met Jeffrey through my brother-in-law, Brian. "What a great fit: He *has* to treat me good—he works for someone in my family!" Jeffrey had the biggest dick I'd ever seen; unfortunately, he *was* the biggest dick I'd ever seen too. He was completely hot but a militant fan of Farrakhan and prone to anti-Semitic remarks. Good sex was nice but I liked the Jews! So long, giant schlong!

John! Oh! John was addicted to recovery groups. I met him when I was just about a size 16. This was the thinnest I'd been in twenty years! On our second date, he looked at me and told me I might wanna lose a few pounds. "Oh, really? A few pounds?" *Get the fuck out!*

Wait a goddamned minute—what had happened here? Somewhere along the line—I don't know where—I had started to like myself! I was losing weight, having fun, and accepting myself too! Who knew *this* was available to Lisa Lampanelli, the chick who once looked *up* to a midget at Pips? I had come a long way from that Sheepshead Bay disaster. And there was no denying black men had helped me get there! I was no longer the fat chick who had to settle! I had never felt this way before! I was on a roll! No one was gonna take that away from me—*ever!*

❖

I remember when it wasn't enough for me to be a guy anymore. Two days after September 11.

Shut out of the city, at my parents' house in Connecticut, I held my own. For two days, I cheered them up, rented silly movies to take our minds off what had happened, and was just happy to be in the house I grew up in. Two days later, after the bridges reopened, I was back at my apartment in New York City. I was alone and I was scared and suddenly I was a girl again.

The second I felt that, I wanted to eat. What was I gonna do? I had come too far to throw it all away. I couldn't go backward! I needed something, though. I needed to be with somebody. I needed to feel safe—I needed to be with somebody big and strong. So I looked up an old friend. I called Andre, my Big Daddy. Andre was the first guy I had felt safe with. And *he* wasn't fattening.

And it was everything I remembered about our first meeting. Still no furniture in his apartment, another forty for him, and two glasses of wine for me. It was great, it was comforting.

So it broke my heart when Andre called me out of the blue the next day and said he was ready for a relationship. I suddenly realized, "Wow, I want one too!"—only not with him.

❀

Every comedian has a favorite joke—a joke he tells when he wants to put himself in a good mood, a joke that really lets him be himself. Mine goes like this: I pick out a black guy in the audience—I'll try for a hot one, but I'll use an Urkel if that's all I've got. I give him a little smile, an up-and-down appraisal, and I say, "I love black guys. I fuck black guys all the time. That's my thing. It ain't by choice. I just haven't lost enough weight to get a white guy to fuck me." Funny, right? It kills every time.

But there's one problem. It's not true.

Now, I'm not one of those die-hard a-holes who thinks every comedian must "speak the truth," so I kept it in my act. But by the time I got down to a size 14, I knew I could get a white guy. But there was a little glitch: I didn't want one.

I was done with booty calls and dead-end flings and I was ready for a *real* relationship with a black man, but I had no idea where to find one. Then I had a thought—goal-oriented gal that I am. I decided to go shopping! And like every good shopper, I made up my list.

The black man I date must:

1. Have a working cell phone;

2. Have a job and an education (at least through the twelfth grade);

3. Not have children, or his children must be grown;

4. Not drink or do drugs;

5. Not be a thug!

That last one was the hardest thing to put on my list. I *loved* dangerous guys and I could finally get them. Thugs were sexy, and they made me feel like I was living some kind of double life—you know, upwardly mobile white gal by day, gangsta bitch by night. But after a year of dating hustlers, bail posters, and parolees, I'd had enough.

My only happily married friend, Darlene, came to my rescue. "Lisa, you should try a nice guy." A nice guy? Yuck! I'd had nice guys all my life. Now that I was used to hot, sweaty, and homicidal, how could I go back to Jared from Subway? My friend looked around like she was a spy and whispered, "Lisa, give a nice guy a chance. Any guy'll thug it up for you in bed if you ask."

Lightbulb! Holy shit! She was right! Even the goofiest, Cosby-est, whitest black guy will do what his woman wants in bed. I've yet to meet a guy who isn't willing to play a little game of *Oz* every once in a while. The difference is, he's playing. And the rest of the time? He's just nice.

Okay, I had my list, I had my goal, and I was ready to shop. But where? I did all my real shopping on the Internet. Being from Connecticut, I knew llbean.com, and amazon.com was where I went for all my self-help and Dr. Phil needs. But shopping for a man online? No fuckin' way! Don't get me wrong: I knew a lot of people used online dating; I'd even heard people found the love of their lives online. But I was Lisa Lampanelli,

Comedy's Lovable Queen of Mean—I might get recognized by one of my hundreds of fans! But at that point, what other choice did I have? I worked seven nights a week and the only guys I met during the day had time to talk because they were unemployed. So, with some fear of being gang-raped in a chat room, I logged on.

Now, you might ask, where does a white gal go when she wants to shop for the perfect black man? Why, she goes to blackmenwhitewomen.com, of course! Seriously, that's a site! I found it one day when I did a Google search for "interracial dating" and there it was! I couldn't believe it! It was like the gates of Africa were opening to me!

God forbid it should be that easy. Turned out blackmen whitewomen.com had about three active members—probably because their phone lines were disconnected—and none of them was ever logged on. I was at a dead end—the only other sites Google gave me were interracial porn sites. Then one day, playing tennis, I was talking to an older Jewish widow who said she met "a very nice man" on kiss.com. Here she was—a woman over fifty-five with a dead husband—and *she* found a match. Shit, if this old bat could find a guy there, so could I!

May I be blunt? Kiss.com's six pages of questions were a pain in the snatch! "Who is your favorite radio host?" "Um, Howard Stern and Garrison Keillor." Yeah, *that* should get me a soul mate. "Do you like English food?" "Uh, no! English people don't like English food!" "To what degree do you like raves?" "Raves! I'm forty! I like them *zero* degrees!!!"

After three hours, I was finally done. For the next few weeks, I don't think I *ever* logged off. As soon as I walked in the door, I cruised around to see who I could talk with and there was always someone there. If there's anywhere that hope springs eternal, it's online.

"Welcome, Comedic1"—that was my online screen name, which, of course, some perv online mistook for Come-Dic 1. "Hello, Comedic1! There are fifty-five men online who match your dating criteria." *Sweet!* Sometimes I chatted with no one and just poked around, other times I had up to eight—that's right, eight—conversations going on at once with black guys all over the tristate area. Sometimes on slow nights, I expanded to Massachusetts, and on one particularly desperate night, New Hampshire.

Pretty soon I began to notice that I was different online. Because it's anonymous, I was being completely myself. And, get this, the guys were trying to impress *me.* That might have been because my picture was smokin'! Almost no one else had a thousand-dollar, retouched headshot posted. *I totally rocked!*

I started racking up the dates. On the first date with each guy, I brought only mace, cleavage, and my list of criteria— phone, job, schooling, no kids. And I met some good ones. Kevin—nice but dumb as a post. Al—manager of a Payless ShoeSource. Need I say more, Star Jones? But, undeterred, I kept plowin' through.

Exactly twenty-four dates later—I will never forget it—I met Greg. Greg was a prince in a Marine uniform. He had everything on my list—and then some! A master sergeant— trust me, that's a good rank—with eighteen years of service, Greg was in the top 3 percent of Marines in physical fitness. Think about that, chew on that, masturbate on that, whatever!

Not only that, Greg had two cell phones, a paid-off house, no children, a brand-new truck, a brand-new car, and would get a healthy pension in two years if he retired at forty. But, said Greg, he wouldn't. Marine-ing to him was a calling. He prided himself on being the first line of defense for the president— the commander in chief. I got off on that . . . plus on the fact that he could kill me with his bare hands. But he wouldn't. Because Greg, ladies and gentlemen, was a gentleman!

For about three months, I was in a state of bliss. Three times a week, I drove out to the Marine base on Long Island and fantasized about my life as a military wife. I would spend my married life wearing pedal pushers, Keds, and a button- down, sleeveless shirt tied at the waist, and a kerchief, a ba- bushka, would hold back my hair. I would be tan and thin, and I would garden while my master sergeant was at war, and I would drive to the PX and buy all sorts of rations and fix- ins. In my old age, I would wait on the front porch—like the mother in *Saving Private Ryan* but without the dead kids— waiting, waiting, in my housecoat and flat shoes, my hair in a bun, until I saw his Jeep round the corner in a cloud of military dust.

Back to reality: For three months, three times a week, Greg and I went out to dinner, to the movies, and cruised around in his truck, and we were having so much fun, I didn't even notice how hard I was trying. After the first ten minutes of each date, the conversation was stilted, but who cared? I was used to thinking on my feet, rallying the troops, coming up with subjects, keeping people entertained—I was a freakin' comic, for chrissakes! Greg talked about going to war—yeah, right, like we were ever gonna go to war! I listened and tried to respond. I didn't care how hard I had to try—this would be worth it! *Greg fit the list—and Kiss said I had a match!!!* But after every date, I was exhausted. Screw it, though! This relationship was *obviously* meant to be—this was gonna work out—*Kiss said I had a match*!

On Easter that year, Greg broke it off. I guess he was sick of trying too. He was polite—the prototypical Marine. He thanked me and said I helped him grow and open up. I cried for a night and saved his message until Verizon's voice mail system deleted it for me twenty-one days later.

Three months later, I was in the middle of putting together an entire apartment-ful of Ikea furniture—and I was in the mood to stay home anyway. Alone. How nineties! But when the Ikea was done—it's not really that hard if you read the freakin' instructions—I had four hours to kill before flying to North Carolina for a gig. Four hours—not enough time to go out, not enough time to go to sleep, but just enough time to cruise online.

Screen name "DarrylKevin" described himself as "Good-Looking"—true—and "Well-built," although all I could see from his photo was his head. By checking the records, I saw that DarrylKevin had read my profile a few times but had never written to me. Sitting there in my bathrobe and dirty hair at two fifteen A.M., I said, "What the hell?" and sent an e-mail to the last guy I would ever date on kiss.com.

When I got to my hotel in North Carolina the next day, an e-mail from DarrylKevin was waiting: "I must have done something right in a previous life to have a woman like you reach out to me." The e-mail contained two phone numbers and a request to please call him *anytime*. "I have looked at your picture often but haven't had the courage to write you." I told you that headshot was magic!

So, I called him. Four hours on the phone the first night, four hours on the phone the next, and four hours on the phone the next—including some hot-and-heavy phone sex. When DarrylKevin offered to come pick me up at the airport—*at Newark, yet!*—I was blown away!

On the airplane from Asheville, North Carolina, to Newark, New Jersey, I couldn't stop smiling. It was June 17, and I knew—*I just knew*—that the minute I stepped off the plane, *my life would be changed forever.* That is absolutely true! Don't laugh at me! Shut up! Yes, I had officially become a romantic! Hey, you try losing sixty pounds, listening to Dr. Joy Browne, and staying a cynic! It's impossible, fucker!

"My life will be changed forever," I thought to myself as the plane landed. I stepped off the flight and walked slowly to the baggage claim area. "My life will be changed forever when I see him—I just know it."

"You must be Darryl." I looked up—way up—and there was this six-foot-five, lean guy with a huge bouquet of flowers (real flowers, not Korean-market crap) with a string of multi-colored ribbons I still have.

"Yep," was all he could say before he gave me the warmest and strongest hug I'd ever gotten. We looked into each other's eyes and—I swear to God—it was like a movie! It was like *When Lisa Met Darkie!* Two girls walked by and gave me the thumbs-up. "You're really lucky," one of them said. "You should have heard what he was saying about you!" Holy crap—he's a freakin' romantic too!

I saw Darryl Kevin almost every day for three years after

we met that night in Newark Airport. Then I saw him less and less.

After moving together to Connecticut, we grew apart. He started going to the gym more, and work-obsessed me? I started gaining more fame and coincidentally more weight. Then he got another girlfriend and forgot to tell me. Was it his fault? Was it my fault? Probably a little of both. But all I know is that every time I dial a phone in the middle of the night to call whoever I'm dating, I hold my breath until they pick up the phone. If they don't pick up—the way Darryl ceased to toward the end of our relationship—the wall goes up. And that wall can't be penetrated, no matter what color the man.

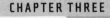
Popping My Cherry:

Important Firsts in the Life of Comedy's Lovable Queen of Mean

ut enough about men, relationships, and chocolate love. Let's talk about the real love of my life, the only thing that's truly fed my soul: comedy.

Every once in a while, I wonder what my life would have been like if I had never started doing comedy. I sometimes think that if I had had a child at the precise moment I first picked up a microphone, I would be sending my eighteen-year-old gay son with a flair for the dramatic off to Parsons right now to hang out with Tim Gunn. I would occasionally gaze out the window of my one-bedroom condo with the linoleum floor and dirty curtains, and before I headed off to my job at Kinko's, I'd put down my *Soap Opera Digest* and reminisce about little gay Bruce's life. Occasionally, when I had a few two many sips of sangria, I would crack open his baby book and look over all the firsts in his life—his first word (definitely "Prada"), his first steps (out of the closet), and his first Il Divo CD.

But alas, dear reader, I have never had the desire to have children—even a little gay boy who ends up the winner of *Shear Genius*. In fact, for almost twenty years, instead of a child, comedy has been my baby. So I have decided to reveal to you in this chapter a list of firsts for my true child: my comedy career. These are the milestones that have meant the most to me as a comedian, and I share them with you here in all their glory.

My First Time Being Recognized

The first time you're recognized on the street is very strange. A stranger approaches you with a weird look on his face and you don't know what he wants. Does he want a quarter or your whole purse? He acknowledges you, and you don't know if you know him from high school, if you owe him money, or if you slept with him in college.

Celebrities who say they hate being recognized on the street are full of it. The pathetic truth is that the unconditional love of a parent or the growing bond with a spouse cannot compete with the thrill of a complete stranger losing his shit at the sight of you. And the first time is the best. You're actually more excited than the person going crazy about you. He's like, "I can't believe it's you." And you're like, "I can't believe you care!" There's hugging and jumping up and down. It's like when your best friend tells you she's getting married—only better, because you're not going to have to buy an ugly dress later. And you don't have to tell her you've slept with her fiancé.

The only thing better than being recognized when you're alone is when you're with your old friends and a stranger walks up and asks for your autograph. It's like, "That's right, bitches. I belong to the world now." These early fan meetings are both validation and hope for the future all rolled up in one. You automatically think to yourself, "I am starting to break through the clutter, and if this person is excited, then there must be more. That means I'm going to be a big star and soon I'll have the money to pay a bodyguard to tell these people to get the fuck away from me." Ah, how good it feels when dreams are coming true.

Although I've been a star in my own mind my entire life, I never thought I'd be recognized on the street. That is, until seven years ago, when I got my first official comedy television credit: Comedy Central's roast of Chevy Chase.

Of course, this was a *huge* break for me, and I looked forward to the show's airdate more than two months after the taping like it was Christmas morning, a trip to Disney World, and Black History Month all rolled into one. As I watched the roast on TV that night in December, I was thrilled to see that although I had performed second-to-last during the taping, I had done so well that I had been moved up to third in the broadcast.

Naturally, I assumed that because this TV broadcast was

so groundbreaking for me, it was equally earth-shattering for the rest of the world. The second the program ended, I jumped up and headed out the door. I was living in New York City at the time and around that time every night, I sent my boyfriend Darryl out just before bed to pick me up a low-fat cookie or protein bar or some other treat that I deluded myself into thinking was good for my diet. But tonight would be different. I was a New Yorker, I was fabulous, and I was just this side of famous. Tonight was the night I was going to the Korean deli myself and I prepared to be well received by all.

I touched up my makeup and hair and headed down to the lobby. I beamed as I got off the elevator, and the doorman nodded hello. Hmmm . . . that was weird. He was treating me just like he had *before* the show aired. But, I quickly remembered, he had an excuse. Of course, he couldn't say, "Great job on the roast." He was on duty, working, without a TV in sight. And besides, there were other people in the lobby and he was much too professional to break my confidentiality. "Good work," I thought to myself, and continued out the door.

It was brisk outside as I walked the half block to the Korean deli on Tudor City Place, and I spotted two people walking their dog near the area's small park. As they approached me, I plastered on my best Miss America smile and prepared to be complimented. I had brought along a pen—in case an autograph hound accosted me (not a Sharpie; I wasn't conceited!)—and I put my hand on it in my pocket so I'd be ready to sign. As the couple passed me, they looked up and nodded politely, just like it was any other night in the enclave east of Second Avenue. Polite? What was that all about? I was braced for some recognition! I had earned it! Hadn't they heard? I was just on Comedy Central! I was the only woman comic to roast that washed-up *Saturday Night Live* alum douche. Goddamn it—didn't they know? *I'd been moved up to third in the order!!!!*

Then I remembered where I was—New York City. New York friggin' City, where there are tons of famous people and where even normal folks—civilians—had perfected the art of being too cool for school or giving them space. That was it, I thought. "These people know who I am—they're just being respectful." I was impressed. I *did* live in a classy part of town.

The next thing I knew, I heard a man calling after me. "Hey, how are you tonight?" "Here it comes," I thought. "Thank God I did my hair and brought my pen." I turned to face him with my cheesiest grin and a generous flip of my hair.

"I'm fine," I said, smiling back at the man, who was dressed all in green. "And you?"

"Good," he said back. "Hey, we were wondering"—he gestured back to where two other guys stood a few yards away—"is that your car? You gotta move it 'cause we can't get to the Dumpster to empty the garbage."

My smile faded and I shook my head. "No, no, it's not my car," I told the New York City sanitation worker. I turned back to my apartment, forgetting all about the cookie I had gone out to fetch.

As I entered the apartment, a little deflated, Darryl jumped up. "Hey, it's the star." That night, I realized that that was all the recognition I was gonna get and all the recognition I probably needed.

In the seven years since that first roast, I've been recognized on the street, in public bathrooms, at airports, and in foreign countries (although I don't think it really counts if it's in Amsterdam and they're so baked they think I'm Bette Midler), and I can't imagine ever getting sick of it. Every time someone asks me if I'm "that comedian" or "Lisa Campanelli" or "that chick who likes the brothas," I get a total kick out of it, like it's the first time. The night of the Chevy Chase roast, I was shocked that no one recognized me. Now, I'm shocked when anyone *does*.

People ask me if I dress incognito at the airport in order to avoid getting noticed. Yes, I do invariably show up for planes in sweats, a ball cap, and zero makeup; that much is true. But while I do dress down to travel, it's not to avoid getting recognized. It's sheer laziness.

My favorite place to get recognized is Starbucks because they always give me free coffee. I had witnessed this firsthand when it happened to Dave Chappelle, and I couldn't believe that a few short years later, it was happening to me. Here I was in Newtown, Connecticut, and some hip, young kid who looked like he attended art school and was in a band said he loved my work. What made it even better was that I was on a first date with a gorgeous black man who looked like the president from that show *24*. Come to think of it, the black guy was probably the accessory the barista needed to place my face. We got free coffee that day, and I left a huge tip as a thank-you, 'cause you know if a black guy thinks you're his ticket to free shit, you're getting a second date.

A few weeks later, I was in another Starbucks, this time in LAX. I had two hours to kill so I wandered into the store for an iced venti skim latte. As I approached the counter, the barista did a double take and squinted at me.

"Hey, haven't I seen you before?"

"Yes." I feigned modesty. "I'm on TV all the time."

He eyed me further and said, "No, that's not it. Didn't you get yelled at once for bringing a dog in here?"

As he turned away to make my drink, I scowled behind his back. He was *so* punished!

Fuck him! I'm glad I forgot my pen.

My First Time Being Heckled

"Bring back the fat chick!"

It was only five words, but it was five words that would change my career—and my life—forever.

The place was one of the thousands of mediocre crab-and-burger joints in any small town that hosts a stand-up comedy show once a week to pull in some extra dough. Since a microphone, a speaker, and a three-by-five-inch patch of floorboard are the only things these restaurants need to mount a show, these rooms were popping up all over in the early nineties, even as the comedy club boom was dying down. And this particular restaurant in Meriden, Connecticut, was no different. The crowd was full of food and half-full of liquor, and had no patience at all for bullshit.

Since I and most of my family are proud to call Connecticut home, I invited my brother and sister-in-law, whom I adore—and at times, idolize—to this, one of my first paid gigs in the area. They hadn't seen me perform in a while and they were excited to have a rare night out, away from their growing family of six kids.

To be honest, my set wasn't my best. Having just started in comedy a year before, I was still finding my legs and hadn't nearly begun to have a cohesive style. Of course, my future as an insult comic and roaster wasn't even a twinkle in my beginner's mind, and I did about fifteen minutes of jokes about my weight (a constant point of controversy in my life), my Italian family, and my current relationship—a mediocre but passable job as the first comic up.

As I introduced the next comic, I breathed a sigh of relief. I had made it through the set without embarrassing myself and my family, and I could go home confident that my brother and his wife would give me a good—if not glowing—review of my set. As I got ready to sit down with them to watch the second comic, who was by that time struggling for laughs, I heard the fateful line that I will never forget: "Bring back the fat chick!"

I froze. That sentence was a double-edged sword. Sure, the drunken creep who yelled it was implying I was funnier than comic number two and that he'd like to see more. But he had called me "fat," a word that every woman from Eve to Eva Braun to Eve Arden to Eve Ensler has feared. I felt my face turn red as the audience, including my family, shifted their gaze to where I stood on leaden feet. In that instant, I made a decision: I was gonna get them before they got me. I was going to be armed and dangerous. I may be the only comedian who has been heckled when she was *off*stage, but in that moment, "Lisa Lampanelli, insult comic" was born.

The next day was a blur of notebook, pen, and pencil as I sat at my parents' kitchen table gathering ammo. Never again would I be caught with my pants down. In fact, I would catch my audience with *its* pants down, and I'd pull 'em down even farther. I'd show them who was boss from the second I stepped onto that stage, and if anyone dared even *think* about heckling, it was on!

Now that I look back, most of the lines I scribbled frantically that day at my parents' house ranged from the mediocre to the horrible. They were lines like "Sir, I don't go to where you work and clean the monkey shit off the windows," "Let me buy you a drink. Waitress, a vinegar-and-water for the douche up front," and "Hey, sir, if your dick was as big as your mouth, you'd be in porno."

While not A-list material by any standard, these lines gave me confidence. See, there's a certain self-assurance in being prepared—hey, did ya ever see an unconfident Boy Scout? No!—and in seventeen years in this business, I can count on two hands the times I've been heckled. Of course, when you're as lovable as I am, this is easy to achieve. Also, I now make sure to make sexual advances on the biggest, hottest security guard before the show. That way, he will crack the skull of anyone who looks at me cross-eyed.

Hey, I may be the fat chick, but I'm the fat chick who puts out. And that's a different story altogether.

My First Time on THE TONIGHT SHOW

The first time you do *The Tonight Show* is a *huge* deal. In the old days when Johnny Carson was there and everybody only had three channels, a good set on *The Tonight Show* would change your life. For me, it served an even more important purpose: It stopped my parents from asking me when I was going to get a real job and quit this monkey business.

Comedy is a strange profession. People who have been onstage two times in their lives have business cards that say "Comedian." Therefore, a comic's entire career is focused on separating himself from the delusional wackos. The difference between being a comic who has done *The Tonight Show* and one who hasn't is the difference between playing basketball at the Y and playing ball in the NBA. You have undoubtedly staked out a career and you can afford to have several illegitimate children.

The best part of being booked on the show is that for a month before your appearance, while talking to other comedians, you can utter the phrase "Yeah, I have to get my jokes ready for *The Tonight Show*." That's the equivalent of saying, "I have to get my pussy waxed for Brad Pitt." It inspires sheer jealousy from everyone who hasn't been there. And, in the end, isn't that what show business is all about?

When people ask if you've been on *The Tonight Show,* they're basically asking you if you're really a comic or just a bank teller who does comedy on the side. To a lot of people, you're not a comic until you've been on *The Tonight Show.* In fact, when I did my first *Tonight Show,* it was one of my greatest honors—even though it wasn't Johnny Carson anymore. Hey, at least it wasn't Conan yet.

Nothing in seventeen years in the business shocked me more than finding out I was being considered as a *Tonight Show* guest. Comics like me—edgy, dirty, C-word-saying beeyotches—didn't appear on *The Tonight Show with Jay Leno* or any network late-night shows, for that matter. Instead, we did BET's *Comic View,* the occasional *Premium Blend,* and Comedy Central after midnight. So, one day in 2006, when my manager called to say that *The Tonight Show* wanted me to appear as a guest on their fabled couch, I thought she had the wrong comic.

"Seriously, they love you, and they want you to come on with Simon Cowell and give him a hard time." Simon Cowell! This was a score! Not only did I *not* have to perform stand-up on the show—a condition I wouldn't bend on since my stand-up did not translate to four minutes of clean and clever material—I could panel with someone who could dish it out *and* take it. I set about writing Simon Cowell insults that were funny but not so insulting that he'd storm off the set with his knickers in a bunch.

I've always been one of those comics who makes it look easy—whether it's a festival audition, a closing set on a roast, or an urban show with an all-black audience—so I knew I had to bring it for *The Tonight Show.* I arrived four hours early for hair and makeup—trust me, hair and makeup on someone over the age of forty takes at least three hours and your own stylist, not the show-provided makeup artist who is used to making models and actresses under thirty look fresh. As I sat in the chair in the number-two dressing room—the number-one dressing room was reserved for Simon—I looked over the notes I'd jotted down after talking to the segment producers a few days before.

First came the specific instructions on how to handle the crowd:

- ❤ INVOLVE THE AUDIENCE!!! TEAM WITH THEM.
- ❤ CONFRONT MOANS—JAY HATES MOANS. SAY "OH COME ON!!!"
- ❤ DON'T MENTION KEVIN'S ERECTION—JAY MAY FEEL IT STEALS HIS THUNDER.

Then came my list of condescending names I'd call Simon in case he interrupted me:

- ❤ "Lemme tell you somethin', Mr. Bean."
- ❤ "Listen, you English fruit."
- ❤ Other British names: Elton, Mr. Belvedere, Niles from *The Nanny*, Mr. Sheffield, Henry Higgins, Monty Python, Benny Hill, Mr. French, Colonel Mustard, "You were great in *My Fair Lady.*"

Below that was my list of surefire shutter-uppers that would cut Simon off at the pass if he interrupted my flow:

- ❤ "Simon, don't be mean to me. I'll give you a lap dance, you'll never walk again."
- ❤ "Hey, Simon, it's my turn. Jeez, he keeps poppin' up like a turd that won't flush. Floater."
- ❤ "Hey, Simon, don't talk to me that way. I'm a freakin' lady. I'm a feminine flower."

💜 "Hey, Simon, I don't need to listen to you. We won the war in 1776—we're independent now."

Last was one final note if all else failed:

💜 Make fun of self.

I've always found that once you are truly prepared, you exude such confidence you don't need your heckler put-downs, your flamethrower, or anything else that is now referred to in comedy as "pulling a Michael Richards." And that night, I was right. From the second I stepped out on the stage and sat down next to Simon, it was flawless. The British guy didn't utter a peep and laughed 'til he nearly fell off the couch, Jay laughed but acted respectively shocked and awed by the entire exchange, and Kevin seemed to love the attention from a white beeyotch with a big ass who was definitely into banging him.

The aftermath was even better than the appearance: a big steak at Morton's, a glowing review from my manager and her boss, and a phone call from all four Blue Collar Comedy guys that can only be described as gushing. (Although I think I heard Ron White drunkenly muttering about a 900 number and saying the word "taint.") The only thing better than the congratulatory phone calls—including a message on my voice mail from my father saying, "Lisa, pick up, pick up," as if I still had an answering machine—was the e-mail the next day asking when I was coming back. Whenever you want, fuckers! I was a *Tonight Show* regular!

My First Time Being Protested

When you're a struggling comic, you hustle so much that you will do almost anything to get to the next level. When you're an open-miker, you want to be getting paid work. When you're a working comic, you want to make enough money to quit your day job. And when you're doing comedy for a living, you need to do something to get famous, noticed, so your tickets can start selling and maybe you can afford to fill up your gas tank and eat more than one meal a day.

Well, since I was always a comic who worked blue—the comedy word for "dirty"—I didn't hold out much hope that I'd ever appear on television. So I always tried to devise ways to get mentioned in the media. First, I thought of doing a slave auction in Times Square during Black History Month, in which I would auction off white girls with big asses to buff black guys as reparations. That would be sure to get me in the papers. However, in September 2002, I landed my first comedy television spot (*The NY Friars Club Roast of Chevy Chase* on Comedy Central), and I was on my way up. The slave auction would have to be shelved.

As controversial as I was, I never got much shit for it. Other than the occasional disgruntled audience member—no more than about one per month (a pretty good rate considering the edgy, racial material I did)—no one sent any hate my way. Sure, there was that one black guy who called in to the radio station in Kansas City who said he was with the NAACP. (Of course, we knew he wasn't when he thought NAACP stood for "Negroes and All Colored People.") And there was that one gay guy in Albany who threatened to picket my show the next night. But he forgave me when I told him he had cute shoes.

Eventually, I started to notice something. Aside from the guys above, the ones who usually got angry at me for my race-based material weren't minorities at all. More often than not, they were self-righteous, liberal white people. You know, the same fucks who turned on Hillary Clinton for having the audacity to campaign. That's right—I noticed it wasn't any of the races who were offended. It was these hypocrites! And the only reason they were angry was they didn't know any minorities. Hey, Linda Liberal! Bang a black guy and then try not to laugh at an ashy-colored ball sack joke! Rent out a room to an Indian couple and then tell me they don't use curry as deodorant. Humor works when it's based in truth. You don't think so? I will give you a hundred bucks for every Jew you can find with a big penis. And I'll double that amount for an Asian.

Not surprisingly, there was one time that I pissed off enough people in one particular town to result in a mass uprising. It was in March 2007, and I was being protested for the very first time.

Let me start, however, by saying that if you're protesting a comedy show, you need a big cock in your ass to loosen it up. It's free speech, bitches! But you know what? When all is said and done, being protested is a compliment. I was honored that people hated me enough to come out and stand in the rain. I wouldn't stand in the rain to end world hunger and these douchebags were standing in the rain to stop a coupla jokes.

But I'm getting ahead of myself. In March 2007, I was pro-tested by the worst group *ever*! No, not black people—I've brought joy to more black men than Kwanzaa. Not Mexi-cans—they were too busy undercutting white workers. And definitely not Asians—they never protest. They just run around the parking lot putting Chinese menus on the pro-testers' windshields. No, folks, the people who were mad at me were—hold on to your Miracle Ears—deaf. But before you say I should have broken their fingers to shut them up, here's the story.

When you book a concert, you call in to the local radio station six weeks in advance to plug your tickets. So, when I found out I was booked at a building on the campus of Roch-ester Institute of Technology in upstate New York, I called ra-dio legend and member of Rochester royalty Brother Wease, with whom I had always had great radio rapport.

Wease, whom I had met at the Just for Laughs festival in Montreal several years earlier, asked me whom specifically I would be making fun of during my show when I came to town. I told him that, as an insult comic, I make fun of everybody—whites, blacks, Jews, Asians, blind, deaf. With that, Wease said something to the effect that the deaf jokes might not go over well in Rochester because there was a college in the area with a predominantly deaf student body.

Without missing a beat, I said something along the lines of, "I don't know about all that, but what I do know is deaf people ain't really deaf. They're retards trying to give themselves an upgrade."

I instantly forgot the whole incident, but apparently the deaf people didn't. I showed up at the hotel in Rochester a month and a half later, and I noticed right on the front page of the local paper a substantial story about the deaf students being up in arms because of my comments on the radio. The next morning, it didn't go away. I showed up at the radio station and there was a TV newswoman chomping at the bit to interview me about that "deaf people are retards" comment. I couldn't believe it! What I had said was absolutely harmless. It wasn't even a joke—it was just a fact. I can't even comprehend that deaf people got mad at me because I made fun of them *on the radio!* Who the fuck told them?

In all fairness, the newswoman did a very balanced job of reporting the story, and I was happy I was allowed to tell my side. Deep down I was sad that the deaf people were angry at me because at every comedian's core is the desperate need to be liked by *everybody*—even retarded deaf people. But I prepared for the show that evening, sending my own camera crew (okay, one of my openers with a digital camera) to the venue in advance to interview audience members and tape the protest.

The good news kept coming: The venue was completely sold out due to the controversy, and the ten or so deaf protesters and their supporters were well behaved and were simply exercising their right to free speech—although when a deaf person speaks, can it really be called "speech"? However, one thing did offend me—the protesters all had picket signs and banners that were not in Braille, so I guess we know these deaf people were really card-carrying racist-against-blind-people douchecocks at heart.

I didn't go away from the incident unchanged. That weekend I learned that I, as a comic, am not for everybody, and if one group has to hate me, I'm glad it's deaf people. They're not exactly my target audience for selling CDs to, so they can lick it.

My First Time in the NEW YORK TIMES

There are all other colleges, and then there is Harvard. There are all other automobiles, and then there is the Cadillac. In media, there are all other newspapers, and then there is the *New York Times*.

The first time you're in the *New York Times* is a big deal. It's the most important newspaper in the world. The *New York Times* is kept in a vault for eternity as a record of our civilization and is not like other papers that are lost once the dog takes a shit on them. It's read by respected people around the world. It's the PBS of newspapers. And it's thicker than a black man's rap sheet.

People lie and say they read the *New York Times* to sound smart. For a stand-up comic to make it into the *Times* means they've reached a significant cultural milestone and not just told a couple racist jokes. That's because the *Times* is all class. There are no ads for Asian massage joints or phone sex in the back of it. You don't get in the *Times* because you're in a show your hippie friend is putting together in the Village.

So since the *Times* is the most respected paper in the world, it's unbelievable to think they would do an article on a know-it-all bitch who gets her jollies by shouting racial slurs. But enough about Martha Stewart. A mention in the *New York Times* is a huge help and really ups the ante when it comes to promotion. A poster looks so much better when you can say,

"The *New York Times* calls Lisa a thought-provoking laugh riot" instead of "Joe Sneadley from the *Mount Kisco Penny Saver* thinks Lisa is just wonderful." So the *New York Times* was a real breakthrough for me. Now if I can just get my picture in the *New York Post* blowing A-Rod, my work will be complete.

Don't get me wrong—even though the *New York Times* is the paper I worship, it is one I have never read. Sure, in my vivid fantasy life, I am one of those classy Upper East Side New Yorkers who lounges over brunch at her favorite outdoor café perusing the ginormous Sunday *Times* over coffee and croissants. Instead, if I'm home in New York on a Sunday morning, I'm in bed 'til at least eleven, then prone on the couch watching *Project Runway* or *Date My Ex: Jo and Slade* marathons until it's time to go to bed again.

But even though I don't read it, I know the value of being *in* it. Making it into the *Times* is getting the crown jewel of media coverage, and I just had to make that happen.

In 2008, the *New York Times* gave me a dream come true—a half-page feature in the Sunday Arts and Leisure section on the day I was attending the Grammy Awards to hopefully pick up my statue in the Best Comedy Album category. It was an amazing piece, with a huge picture, and was completely factually accurate and complimentary.

However, this wasn't my first mention in the *Times*. That one had come ten years earlier, in a small article that held even more weight for me. I'll explain.

Around the year 2000, I was appearing at a weekly all-women show at the sadly-now-closed Rascals Comedy Club in West Orange, New Jersey. In its heyday, the club hosted lots of big-name talent on the weekends, but Tuesdays were reserved for "special shows." No, not shows with retards—shows with themes. After watching me a few times, the Magnuson brothers, who owned the club, gave me my own show every Tuesday with the catch being it had to feature only women comics.

Now, I've always hated theme shows, but this was a chance to headline one of the best clubs on the East Coast every week, build a following, and work out more than an hour of material. One week, a *Times* reporter who covered the arts and entertainment scene in New Jersey showed up to do a piece and I not only manipulated myself into the paper but landed myself a nickname that stuck.

See, I never wanted to be a comic who didn't have a moniker. I wanted to have a tagline—a way for people to introduce me onstage, a handle that would make people remember me even when my actual name slipped their minds. One of my openers and I had come up with "Comedy's Lovable Queen of Mean." I didn't want to be known as simply the "Queen of Mean" since Leona Helmsley already had dibs on that for all the wrong reasons. And I wanted the word "lovable" to appear somewhere in there to show that even though I was an insult comic, I meant no harm to people and they wished me no harm in return. And of course, I wanted the word "comedy" in there so the gays didn't think I was a drag act.

I sized up the reporter, who seemed to be a semi-newbie. I mean, c'mon—covering arts and entertainment for the Sewage State had to be on the bottom rung of the *Times* hierarchy. So I set about planting my nickname in print.

"They call me 'Comedy's Lovable Queen of Mean,'" I told the reporter. I looked at her reporter's notebook and saw upside down that she had written down "Queen of Mean." I corrected her, "No, it's '*Comedy's Lovable* Queen of Mean'— it's a lot different, you know? Nobody gets mad at me," I said. She quickly added the two words, and when the article came out the following Sunday, I had a new nickname and it stuck. Thank God! It was so much better than my original show business moniker, "That Fat Bitch Who Cusses."

So now, whenever a reporter asks me why I call myself that, I matter-of-factly say, "The *New York Times*—they said that about me. Why?" Nothing like being anointed by the best newspaper in the world—even though it was engineered by li'l ol' L.L. Incidentally, that reporter was later indicted for leaking CIA secrets in the Scooter Libby trial.

My First Limo Ride
. . . .

The first limo ride is the bomb. And I'm not talking about you and twenty of your friends renting one to play "smell my finger" on prom night. I'm talking about the first time a comedy club sends one for you at the airport and then keeps it at your service all week long. It is a little odd, though, being dropped off at the movies in a limo, especially when you're by yourself and you're going to see *Shrek 3*. It's worth it, though, if the comedy club is paying.

It's actually shocking the first time a club sends a limo for you because it sneaks up on you. The year before, they refused to pay your taxi fare from the airport and they put you up at the shittiest hotel that didn't specialize in crack whores. And suddenly since you started making money for them, not only do they get you a limo, they also have to have bottled water and fruit trays in the greenroom. That's the first sign you've made it: when a club owner is kissing your ass.

Now, I have never been big on stretch limos—they're difficult to get in and out of and embarrassing to ride around in. But early on, the stretch limo sends the right message. Nothing says, "Hey, club owner! Yeah, you—the guy who last year didn't let me order a steak! The tables have turned!" like a stretch limo. The only thing better is farting and having the owner too fearful of offending you to even plug his nose. Quite honestly, I usually try to combine the experiences so the greedy bastard can't escape.

All in all, your first limo ride is awesome but you feel a little weird. It's not someone's wedding; it's all for you and you're just going to a comedy show. You remember going to comedy shows in your '74 Duster, and now you have a car and a driver.

And there's a lot of pressure—you want to be totally nice to the driver and not have him think you're an asshole, so it's like, do I turn on the TV? How loud should I play the music? Is it okay if I take one of the bottles of water with me? Will he think I'm a bitch if I ask him not to talk to me?

Then comes the issue of tipping. Now that I'm a bona fide huge celebrity, the promoters hire high-end transportation companies that figure in the tip, presumably to protect the driver from getting stiffed by cheap Jew producers and black professional athletes who think "gratuity" is just the name of their baby's mama. But in the old days, the limo companies the clubs hired for me didn't include the tip, so the question became "How much?" Of course, I didn't want the driver to think I was a cheap cunt and tell stories about me. Plus Wynonna

Judd had probably given him a hundred yesterday when all I have is a twenty and a five. Great! Now I'll be up there on his list of twats, along with Donna Summer and Paul Anka.

The first time you take a limo, you're kind of embarrassed 'cause you have the sort of "What have I done to deserve this treatment?" mentality. God forbid you inconvenience the driver. You're okay with him dropping you off three blocks away from the gig so he doesn't have to make a U-turn. But pretty soon, that thoughtfulness wears off, and you start bossing him around like you're Meryl Streep in *The Devil Wears Prada*. These days, unless my driver has my coffee the way I like it (venti iced decaf latte, skim) and the car's temperature at exactly 72, his boss is getting a call. And he better not give me shit about hopping out to pick up my dry cleaning. My promoter's paying you for your time—make it happen.

My first limo ride was during a series of gigs at the Foxwoods Casino in Mashantucket, Connecticut. It wasn't a stand-up gig, per se. I was hired to act in a corporate training seminar and was being paid more than I'd ever been paid before—almost $1,000 per day. As a perk, the other actors and I got to eat at the employee cafeteria *for free* and they had a limo pick me up every day for two weeks at my parents' house in Connecticut. Nothing says "I've made it" like having a stretch limo pick you up before the crack of dawn at your parents' house where you're staying rent-free so you can save money as a struggling comic.

Since I had to arrive at Foxwoods by around seven A.M., it was still dark out when the limo picked me up, but the neighbors in my parents' suburban town never failed to notice. Lights in the three houses that surrounded my parents' would pop on as the limo pulled up and go abruptly off as we pulled out of the driveway. My mother would wave good-bye every morning from the open front door, and before we'd turned the corner, I'd be off to sleep.

Now, if you've ever tried to sleep in a stretch limo, you know it's impossible to fall asleep and stay asleep lying across the seats. One quick turn or lane change, and you're in a pile on the floor. This happened to me the first few days, so after day three, I had a brilliant idea. I asked the driver if the limos were vacuumed after each use, and he assured me they were. So, in the me-sized nook on the floor of the limo, I spread out my coat and curled up like a cat. I slept the entire hour and a half to Foxwoods each and every morning on the floor of the car with the sounds of ice and thick crystal decanters of mystery liquor clinking and tinkling in my ear.

I often think back to those days at Foxwoods when I was first treated as if I'd made it and it makes me smile. Of course, today, I prefer a high-end Audi or Mercedes when I'm driven, or when I'm feeling particularly black, I like an Escalade. The cars may have changed, but one thing hasn't—I still lay on the floor. I don't want my opening act to see me and ask for a ride back to the hotel.

Oh, and I hope in my next book you'll hear about the first time I took my private jet and how I'm already over it.

My All-Time Favorite: My First Time on **HOWARD STERN**

The first time you do the Howard Stern show, you're a nervous wreck. *Everybody* listens to Stern. He is the King of All

Media and can make or break your career like Johnny Carson used to in the old days.

The first time on Howard Stern is terrifying, because you don't know what's going to happen. It's like your first time with a Latino—it could be fantastic, or you could wake up with a sore ass and all your valuables stolen. It could easily go either way.

That's because you're not doing a comedy set on Howard's show. You are going to have a really personal interview, with questions as intimate as those in a shrink's office. Only unlike at the shrink's office, you feel pressure to make it funny *and* it's on the radio with millions of people listening. And the people listening can be brutal.

Howard's audience members are like pit bulls. If they sense Howard likes you, they nuzzle right up and sniff your crotch. (I wish I were talking figuratively, but anyone who has ever dealt with Richard Christy knows that I'm not.) But if they sense Howard doesn't like you, they attack. Howard's audience is the only group of people I know who will pay good money to see a comedy show just because they want to fuck it up.

Plus, it's so early in the morning, you're not even awake. You go to the studio and it's still dark outside. Simple yes-or-no questions are confusing at six A.M., let alone a Stern zinger. You're worried about what Howard is going to ask you. He always digs deep into people, and when you dig into me, there are a lot of things to pull out of my vagina.

But before you say, "Well, at least it's radio, not television," think again. Times have changed. Used to be you could be as ugly as you wanted on the radio, but now there are TV cameras in almost every studio—especially Howard's—so you have to look good and you can't pick your nose. Plus every woman wants Howard, the arbiter of all things attractive, to tell her she looks good. Or at the very least try to get her to take her top off once.

The biggest compliment Stern can give you is being asked to stay for the news. It's the same as when comedians were called to Johnny's couch—it means you're in. I could care less about the news, but I'd sit through Baba Booey's colonoscopy to get in with the king.

I know what you're thinking: "That's a lot of pressure." Well, with me, add on even more. Not only did I have Howard, his staff, his listeners, and the early morning hour to deal with, I had to deal with the fact that Howard is my *hero*. To fail on his show would be like shooting an air ball in front of Michael Jordan. Here I was appearing on his show on K-Rock, on terrestrial radio (*not* on no-holds-barred Sirius satellite radio), and this show would not only impact my career, it could seriously affect my self-esteem and ego. It's one thing to go on a show and have a desire to kill. It's quite another to appear on a show and want to kill plus get the approval of the man you've had on a pedestal for the past quarter-century. To blow it here would be like farting on your wedding night.

Being on the Stern show had been a dream of mine since the day I started comedy. But until I did the roast of Chevy Chase, I didn't feel like I had earned the right to be there. Chevy, though, was, at the time, a sworn enemy of Stern and had been such a scowling, sulky, humorless bitch at the Comedy Central roast, I thought this was the hook I needed to get on Howard's show.

After the taping of the roast, I left a message for producer Gary "Baba Booey" Dell'Abate, telling him I had appeared on the roast and wanted to come on Howard's show and tell all the jokes I did about Chevy, plus give them the inside scoop about how Chevy behaved that night. When Howard hates someone, he *really* hates him, so something told me I'd get a call back. Within two days, Gary called and booked me for the following week.

So the pressure was on. First things first, I booked a hair and makeup artist to come over to my little studio in Manhattan at five A.M. since I had to arrive at K-Rock by eight thirty. I enlisted my gay opening act, Wendel, to come with me for moral support, to lighten the mood as he always did, and to program his tape player to record the show on cassette so I had it forever.

Then I set about figuring out what to talk about on the show. Gary had told me Howard wanted to hear the Chevy roast jokes and stories. In fact, ever since my first appearance, it's become a tradition for me to give Howard a preview of my jokes for the roasts, plus give him the exclusive on the ones that don't make it into the broadcasts. But what else should I talk about? I wanted to stay on as long as possible, and Chevy would take up about fifteen minutes tops. I mean, this wasn't 1982—the guy wasn't that interesting anymore.

Luckily, I bumped into comedian Jim Florentine, a friendly, affable, and funny guy who had made his way into the Stern inner circle of guests. Jim is probably the nicest guy in the business because he is genuinely happy for people who get ahead and he shares any knowledge that he has openly and freely. At the Comedy Cellar the night before Stern, Jim said he'd heard I was doing the show and gave me some valuable advice: By the time you're done at the studio, make sure you leave Howard with one hook about yourself, Jim said, what you're known for, so you're memorable to him and you stand out in his mind. At the time, I'd just started talking about having a black boyfriend, so Jim advised me to lead with that. The hook had an added benefit, Jim said, because Howard loves to talk about sex. Jim guaranteed that this would really tickle him.

The next morning, with my hair and makeup done, I headed up to the studio in a cab with gay Wendel, armed with all my notes on Chevy, my roast script, my jokes about banging black guys, and a few insults about other cultures in case Howard asked me about being an insult comic as well. I was wearing my blond hair in the shoulder-length suburban housewife flip that I had sported at the roast, a light-blue cashmere sweater set from Bloomingdale's, and a long navy tube skirt from Eileen Fisher. My weight was at my all-time comedy low, and I felt great, albeit nervous.

As we were buzzed into the studio, we walked by a short-ish Italian guy who I later found out was Ronnie the limo guy. He didn't smile but nodded hello. At the time, I won-dered if he was familiar with my comedy and hated me. Gary came out and ushered Wendel and me into the greenroom, an area complete with an animal-print couch and hot-pink pillows. Wendel joked about how many bare penises must have flopped around on the couch, but I was too busy looking over my notes to listen or fake a laugh. Besides, he'd made the exact same joke in the taxi and whenever we shopped at Macy's.

Before too long, Gary said it was time, and truly almost everything else is a blur. I was seated on a large couch across from Robin in her news booth, so I could direct most of my comments and jokes to her. Howard was to my right, so I tried as hard as I could to face both of them at the same time. At my feet were my notes, which I whipped out and looked over during the commercials, since Howard was busy talking to his assistants and Gary whenever the show broke and Robin was in the booth. I figured it was better to look busy than to sit there idly staring at the walls of the studio.

Here are the things I *do* remember about the appearance:

- Howard was a perfect gentleman. He said I looked nice, and when Joey Boots, a Stern Wack Packer whom I'd had a brief fling with, called in and said I wasn't attractive, Howard said, "She's not bad. What're you talking about?" Score one for my self-esteem.

- During one of the few commercial breaks during which Howard wasn't conducting business, he asked me if I went to a shrink. I said I did, and he said, "Good," and told me that he too was going to a shrink, only he went four times a week. I remember thinking, "I wish I could afford that."

- After asking me about being an insult comic, Howard asked me if I said "nigga" onstage. No, I told him, I used the word "nigger," and pronounced the word with a hard "R" at the end. He was fascinated and I explained my philosophy on treating everyone equally at my show. I told him that if I'm gonna say "kike" to Jews, I should, by rights, say the N-word to black people. Howard seemed impressed.

After about a half hour, my segment came to a close. I sat there bracing for the worst, and Howard said those cherished seven little words: "Can you stick around for the news?"

I said, "Absolutely." And I did.

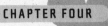

CHAPTER FOUR

Mixed Nuts Roasting on an Open Fire

S ome people were born to be great parents. Others were born to find cures for diseases like cancer and the AIDS. I, however, know I was born with a higher purpose in mind: I, Lisa Lampanelli, was born to roast.

Roasting is my calling, and if I look back on my life, even at an early age, I can remember knowing I could make fun of people and have them take no offense. To me, poking fun or roasting means you can say whatever you want about someone because you clearly don't mean a word of it. And as a kid,

I could make my mom smile even when she was having a bad day by taking little jabs at her and the rest of the family.

It's not like my history of insulting people is unblemished. My stomach turns when I remember referring to someone in my dorm at Syracuse University as a "kike"—probably not a great idea, considering it had a large enough Jewish population to be referred to as "Syracuse Jew-niversity." And there was that unfortunate incident with an Asian guy—I'm not sure which kind—when I called him a "Chinaman" and I ended up on the business end of one of his martial arts throws. But, remember, these things took place in college, where all things are liberal and nobody cares if you mean it or not.

Twenty years later, I get paid to make fun of people, and it's nowhere more appreciated than at the roasts. Whether on Howard Stern's radio show, on Comedy Central in front of millions, or at the closed-door, thousand-seat, no-reporters-allowed Friars Club, a roast is my time to shine. All you need is a microphone, a podium upon which to place your script, a pen so you can cross out similar jokes by guys who go before you, and a very open-minded, non-self-serious individual as the guest of honor. Other than that, there are no rules, and political correctness is out in the parking lot where the spics are breaking into the roasters' cars.

Below, in no particular order, are my recaps of some of the roasts I've done, beginning with the one that started the ball rolling for me and the reason I have a career to this day, the Friars Club roast of Chevy Chase.

NY Friars Club Roast of **CHEVY CHASE**

* *

Date broadcast: December 1, 2002
Roastmaster: Paul Shaffer of *The Late Show with David Letterman*

Fun Facts About the Roast:

❤ In an interview in *Entertainment Weekly,* Chevy Chase said this roast was the absolute worst experience of his life.

❤ Comedian Kevin Meaney, who has since enjoyed a lengthy run in the musical *Hairspray* on Broadway, bombed so hard at the roast, he was cut out of the telecast.

❤ As a result of the roast, I was given my first shot on the Howard Stern show and was able to snag my amazing manager and personal appearance agent, with whom I still work today. This could be an industry record for longevity in such a relationship.

❤ Roastmaster Paul Shaffer pulled me aside at the after-party and told me I was the only roaster Chevy liked because I did not reference his drug-addled past.

❤ People on the dais included tennis superstar John McEnroe with his wife, singer Patty Smyth of Scandal; talk-show host and plastic-surgery victim Sally Jessy Raphael; Chris Meloni and Dean Winters of *Oz* fame; and still-cute-as-a-button actress Martha Plimpton.

Paul Shaffer's Introduction

"Lisa Lampanelli has been called the cross between Don Rickles and Archie Bunker, but in fairness to Lisa, she has a much younger-looking penis. Not thicker, just younger. Here she is—Friar Lisa Lampanelli."

Joke I Chickened Out of Doing

"Sally Jessy Raphael is a very dedicated professional. Every day, she has her stylist drive all the way in from Connecticut to do her makeup. No offense, Sally, but by the looks of you lately, I think the commute is affecting his work."

Favorite Joke of My Set

"Chevy, your beautiful wife, Beverly D'Angelo, in those *Vacation* movies. What sparks flew between those two, huh? I haven't seen chemistry like that since Rosie O'Donnell poked Tom Cruise with her strap-on. Speaking of Rosie O'Donnell, it's nice to see you here . . . Oh, that's Freddie Roman."

NY Friars Club Roast of DONALD TRUMP

Date: October 15, 2004
Private, closed-door roast/not for broadcast
Roastmaster: Regis Philbin

Fun Facts About the Roast:

❤ The Donald Trump roast marked the one hundredth anniversary of the legendary Friars Club.

❤ Because of my performance at the Chevy Chase roast two years prior, my parents were seated at the front of the room with Richard Belzer's and Geraldo Rivera's wives, instead of in the back of the room with the kitchen help.

❤ When he got up for his closing remarks, Donald Trump was extremely entertaining and funny, and I left the roast a huge fan. During the Don King roast the following year, Trump served as roastmaster and was smug, unfunny, and even more unlikable than you'd think. I left unimpressed.

❤ Afraid of offending "the Donald" with my material that was edgy even by roast standards, the Friars Club asked me to do the roast in character as Esther Rabinowitz, who lost her virginity to Donald Trump. After having sex with Trump, "Esther" was so horrified by her experience with the "short-dicked egomaniac" that she renounced sex for good and joined a nunnery. I appeared in a full Roman Catholic nun's habit, complete with huge wooden swinging cross. The Esther Rabinowitz character was first seen earlier that year when I had appeared at a tribute in honor of Friars Club dean Freddie Roman.

❤ Seated on the dais next to me was Artie Lange, who consumed a huge amount of alcohol during the lunch. I was completely sure that he would bomb because of his great ingestion of inebriants, but from backstage where I was changing into my nun's habit, I heard him *crushing* with the best set of the day thus far.

♥ I had heard a rumor before the roast that comedian Susie Essman had requested to sit next to CBS president Les Moonves during the roast. Unfortunately, Les canceled at the last minute, so I couldn't do the following joke: "Look at Susie Essman, sucking up to Les Moonves. She's pitching her new sitcom. It's a companion show to *Desperate Housewives*. It's called *Desperate Whore Comic*."

♥ Other notable folks on the dais included actor Danny Aiello, Dominic "Uncle Junior" Chianese, Regis producer Michael Gelman, mob princess Victoria Gotti, Isaac Hayes, artist LeRoy Neiman, the lovely Jerry Orbach, Vincent "Big Pussy" Pastore, Michael Spinks, and Abe "Yep, I'm Still Alive" Vigoda.

Regis Philbin's Introduction

"Donald, we have a very special guest for you today—something of a surprise. We have a young lady who was one of your, I think, it was your very first date you ever had in Queens. And it is so nice your first girlfriend has joined us now. Esther Rabinowitz, ladies and gentlemen, Esther Rabinowitz."

Joke I Didn't Do at the Roast

"Donald Trump is worth millions and millions of dollars and owns countless buildings all over the world. For the love of God, Donald! Just spend the $8,000 for the penis enlargement and end it." I did not cut this joke out because I was afraid it would offend Mr. Trump. I cut it out because it didn't really seem to fit the character. I used it a few years later on one of the Stern roasts about Howard since he is constantly joking about his small penis. Howard loved the joke.

Favorite Joke of My Set

It's a tie between:

"I have to wrap this up because Regis has to go early. He has to talk Kathie Lee Gifford off a ledge. I haven't seen a career move that doomed since Al Sharpton ran for president. No offense, Reverend Al, but at least Kathie Lee only made that mistake once."

And:

"Truth be told, the reason I left Donald Trump was because he would not marry me unless I signed a prenuptial agreement that said he would keep all the money and I would get all the furniture. Has anyone seen how tacky this guy lives? In his foyer, he has a statue of David naked—which would be classy if it wasn't David Hasselhoff. Let's just say, 'gaudy, fake, and vulgar' isn't just his taste in women. (Audience moans.) Bring it on, bitches! I am a fuckin' nun! Laugh or I will kick you in the cunt!"

NY Friars Club Roast of JERRY LEWIS

* *

Date: June 9, 2006, noon
Private, closed-door roast/not for broadcast
Roastmaster: Richard Belzer

Fun Facts About the Roast:

♥ I was shocked when I heard that Jerry Lewis had specifically requested me for his roast, the third one honoring him at the Friars Club. In some highly publicized remarks, Lewis had made it clear he didn't think women comics were funny, so when I was asked to do the roast (he had seen my appearance with Simon Cowell on *The Tonight Show with Jay Leno*), I jumped at the chance.

♥ The roast began at noon, as all Friars Club roasts do, now that they are no longer partnered with Comedy Central. I told the Friars Club that I could not appear at the roast unless I was able to leave no later than one P.M. so I could make my previously scheduled gig that evening in Kansas City. After doing what might have been my best roast set ever, I hugged Jerry, shook Robert De Niro's hand, and beat it out to the limo to grab my flight to KC. I burst into tears in the car because I could not enjoy the roast aftermath, which is always my favorite part.

♥ On the way to my gig in KC, the plane was delayed two hours, so I was forced to get changed for the show in the airport and do my hair and makeup in the tiny airplane bathroom. As I was finishing up, the smoke detector in the bathroom started to shriek—it seems my hairspray had set it off. I assured the stewardess that I didn't smoke, and I proceeded to show up almost two hours late for my gig and luckily was not arrested for tampering with the smoke detection equipment on the plane.

- Jerry Lewis suffered a heart attack less than two days after the roast. I joke that I like to think I am partially responsible for it.

- Sandra Bernhard, self-serious dyke, gave me the finger whenever I made a joke about her and sat with her arms folded during my entire set, proving once again that she's a cunt.

- People on the dais included Martin Scorsese, Robert De Niro, *Soprano* Vincent Curatola, Chris Elliott, rapper/actor Ice-T, scourge to his own people Don King, Broadway cornholer Nathan Lane, professional questioner James Lipton, Michael McKean, Vinnie Pastore, Joe Piscopo, and Steven Van Zandt.

Richard Belzer's Introduction

"Lisa Lampanelli is known as the Queen of Mean. You would be mean too if the last time you got laid was on a pool table in Newark. Lisa got into trouble last year with the IRS because, on her tax return, she forgot to list her occupation as cunt. She has a deal with Fox for a TV series next season. She is one of the funniest women I have ever seen and you will see right now; please welcome Lisa Lampanelli."

Joke I Chickened Out of Doing

"Don't worry, Jerry. It's almost over. I don't mean the roast."

Favorite Joke of My Set

"Man! Look at all these guinea greaseball actors—or as Martin Scorsese calls them, 'My bitches.' I haven't seen this many Italians in one place since Free Cannoli Day at OTB."

Roast of GENE SIMMONS for GENE SIMMONS: FAMILY JEWELS on A&E

* * * * * * * * * * * * * * * * * * * *

Date broadcast: June 15, 2008
Roastmaster: Jeffrey Ross

Fun Facts About the Roast:

- The comedy rock band Metal Skool got more laughs than most of the roasters combined.

- The most disorganized and sweatiest roast I've ever attended, the Gene Simmons roast made me yearn for the days of even the craziest of Comedy Central roasts. When it started more than an hour late, I braced myself, but it ended up being hands-down the most fun roast I've ever attended, due mostly to the jovial attitude of Gene and his amazing family.

- Comics who performed but didn't make it to air were Ralphie May and Paul Mooney. I was not surprised Ralphie was left out (roasts aren't his thing), but Paul Mooney did a good job. I think it was a black thing.

❤ For over an hour in the downstairs bar before the roast, *Jackass*'s Steve-O was slamming drinks. So it was no surprise that he was wasted by the time the taping began. Sitting in the top row on the stage, he whipped out his penis and peed on the rug and into a glass on the stage. Danny Bonaduce, who, by comparison, seemed tame, complained, and Steve-O was promptly removed.

❤ Criss Angel, another A&E "personality," sent a taped message that was so devoid of laughs and content, it didn't make it to air. I was bummed because, since his tape didn't make it to air, my following joke had to be cut out of the broadcast: "Criss Angel! What an annoying douche! Criss Angel is so irritating, when I watch his show, I always root for the wood chipper."

❤ The way I ended up on the Gene Simmons roast is that I own a house at Canyon Ranch health spa in Tucson, where Shannon Tweed and her sister vacation quite a lot. One day at dinner when I was eating by myself, I heard, "Is that my husband's favorite comic?" To which I replied, "Yes, it is." The two women and their daughters sat and ate dinner with me, and I told Shannon I thought Comedy Central should roast Gene at some point because he seems to have a great sense of humor about himself. A few days later, a producer on *Family Jewels* called and asked me to appear on the roast.

❤ Also overheard at the Canyon Ranch dinner table (and I paraphrase): "Gene isn't here. He was supposed to come but he had the opportunity to make money, so he did it. You know, he's a Jew."

Jeffrey Ross's Introduction
"Our final roaster tonight is an equal opportunity offender—your ears and your eyes. Here she is—batting cleanup, baby. The Queen of Mean, the big double L, Lisa Lampanelli."

Favorite Joke About Me That Night
"We are here to honor a man that taught me that even if you are not talented, you can still put on a lot of makeup, over-market yourself, and make it. Lisa Lampanelli, take a bow." —Jim Norton

Joke I Couldn't Do Because of a No-Show
"I'm glad to see Richard Pryor made it here tonight. Oh, wait, that's Downtown Julie Brown. Yikes! Look at you, Julie! I had no idea the 'Downtown' in your name was short for 'Downtown Newark.' Speaking of nasty old-ass black pussy, Paul Mooney is here."

Joke I Chickened Out of Doing
"You're an ugly, ugly man, Gene. But I gotta hand it to you. You keep trying. I loved the episode of *Family Jewels* where you got plastic surgery. Look at you! I'm not saying your surgery was a failure, but I can honestly say that Kanye West's mother got better results."

Roast of **SANTA CLAUS** for **LARRY THE CABLE GUY'S CHRISTMAS SPECTACULAR** on VH1

Date broadcast: December 5, 2007
Roastmaster: Larry the Cable Guy

Fun Facts About the Roast:

- My custom-made Mrs. Claus outfit, which cost me exactly $0, netted me more complimentary e-mails than my Grammy Awards dress, my *Dirty Girl* Comedy Central special dress, and my Flavor Flav roast dress combined. The cost of those dresses? Over $12,000 total.

- George Wendt, who played Santa Claus, was in a near-panic at rehearsal the day before the roast because he didn't like the roast jokes written for him by the staff of the special. I immediately got the producer to kick in a few thousand dollars to have four professional roast writers I know write him killer Santa rebuttal jokes in six hours flat.

- Flavor Flav's youngest baby (one of nine, I believe) attended the taping of the special. The baby's mother was very pleasant and clearly in love with Flav. Who can blame her?

- The thigh-high patent-leather, five-inch-heel, lace-up platform boots I was supposed to wear with my sexy Mrs. Claus outfit had to be shelved because my foot simply could not bend that high at the arch. Having not packed any high heels for myself that week, I scrambled around backstage trying to find someone wearing size-10 black pumps. Luckily, one of the wardrobe women had a pair that fit, so as she watched barefoot from the wings, I performed in her Manolo Blahniks. Sadly, I had to give them back.

Larry the Cable Guy's Introduction

"I would like to introduce somebody now who knows Santy Claus better than anybody. Please give it up for somebody who's given it up for just about everybody else: Mrs. Santy Claus."

Favorite Joke About Me That Night

"I see Mrs. Santa is sitting over there. I'm not saying she's ugly . . . but if I checked into a hotel with her, I would have to put out the 'Please Disturb' sign." —Tony Orlando

Favorite Joke of My Set

It's a tie between:

"Sex with Santa is kind of like Christmas morning—it only happens once a year, it goes way too fast, and when it's over, there's a huge mess to clean up."

And:

"Look at you, Santy! You big tub o' crap! Who ever told you that red was slimming? I hate that red suit. When Santa lays on a white sheet, it looks like the Japanese flag."

Roast of **ARTIE LANGE** for ***THE HOWARD STERN SHOW**, Howard 100, Sirius Satellite Radio

* *

Date broadcast: June 9, 2006
Roastmaster: Bob Levy

Fun Facts About the Roast:

- The Howard Stern roasts are easily the most no-holds-barred roasts since the nontelevised Friars roasts of thirty years ago. There is no censoring, no editing, and no one is left out, even the King of All Media himself.

- The roasts are held at the Sirius Satellite Radio studios on Avenue of the Americas in New York City. There is a small, by-invitation-only studio audience that sometimes consists of contest winners or sponsors and Stern show regulars like Angry Black or the King of All Blacks.

- The Howard Stern roasts are the only roasts where microphones are stuck in the face of various folks on the dais as they are being made fun of so they can interrupt the person roasting—a huge source of frustration for any professional roaster.

- Since this roast took place the evening before it was to be broadcast, the roast had a more special and looser feel to it than roasts held in the morning.

- This was the most roast-intensive two-day period of my life. Having roasted Artie that evening, I headed back to the New York Hilton where I was staying,

only to wake up early the next day for the roast of
Jerry Lewis at noon.

Bob Levy's Introduction

"We got Lisa Lampanelli coming up. She only dates black guys.
Her career must be going well to be able to afford all that bail
money. Let's have a hand for my friend Lisa Lampanelli."

My Favorite Introduction of the Roast

"The next person is a smelly cunt that wears bad makeup and
has to yell 'nigger' to be funny. And it's not Lisa Lampanelli.
Let's have a hand for my friend Yucko the Clown."

Favorite Jokes About Me That Night

"Lisa has had more black hands on her snatch than the hood
of a cop car." —Sal the Stockbroker

"Black guys shoot into Lisa like she's a nightclub with a 'no
sneakers' policy." —Colin Quinn

Favorite Joke of My Set

"Artie Lange is a huge star. You know you're big when Andrew
Dice Clay takes the time to send a tape."

My Fake-Sincere Ending

"Artie, I suppose what I'm trying to say is that yes, Artie, I
am proud of you . . . Every morning you provide people with
a much-needed service, you get them going in the morning.
Each day, millions of people listen to you while they're getting
ready for work. Wow! They get to be entertained by you and
take a shit at the same time."

Roast of **DANIEL CARVER** *for THE HOWARD STERN SHOW,* Howard 100, Sirius Satellite Radio

. . . .

Date broadcast: March 29, 2006
Roastmaster: Bob Levy

Fun Facts About the Roast:

💜 This was the tensest roast that I, and probably anyone else attending, had ever witnessed. Daniel Carver wore his full Klansman outfit and was put in Robin Quivers's glass booth since he needed to be separated from the various minorities on the dais.

💜 This roast was proof that the old adage "We only roast the ones we love" is the way to conduct such an event. Since Daniel Carver—and most Klansmen, Nazis, etc.—are hated across the board, it is almost impossible to do an entertaining roast because the jokes contain none of the irony of making fun of someone who is well liked.

💜 Most of the black comedians on the dais had never roasted anyone before, and this showed in their lack of preparation. While all the comics who were there are inherently funny, the lack of specially written material was the final nail in the coffin of this roast.

💜 I had a very uncomfortable conversation with Daniel Carver in the greenroom after the roast, where he said he was right about "those people." I am assuming he meant blacks.

Bob Levy's Introduction

"We have Lisa Lampanelli coming up. She would do anything to get a black guy to fuck her. I heard she dips her tampons in barbecue sauce. She has fucked more blacks than slavery. She is known as the female Don Rickles. The difference is I would let Don Rickles blow me when I was drunk."

Favorite Jokes About Me That Day

"Those brothers love Lisa's pussy because that's where they hide the television sets." —Sal the Stockbroker

"I wish I had a dime for every time I get mistaken for Lisa Lampanelli." —Artie Lange

Sweetest Things Ever Said About Me at a Roast

"Lisa, I don't care if you look like that. All I need is a female with a heartbeat." —Hot chocolate comic Corey Holcomb

"Give it up for my lady that fucks black men. I love you. Please be with me. I will move you up like Weezie. If the shit don't work out, you got to be Florence and clean for the other bitch, but you still in the house." —Earthquake

Favorite Joke of My Set

"We are here today to honor KKK representative Daniel Carver. You and I have a lot in common. We both like to screw the black man. Of course, when you do it, they get lynched. When I do it, all I get is a rash and chapped lips."

The Comedy Central Roast of **PAM ANDERSON**

Date broadcast: August 14, 2005
Roastmaster: Jimmy Kimmel

Fun Facts About the Roast:

💜 No news here: Courtney Love misbehaved. But what you might not know is that she misbehaved more than viewers saw. Taping had to be stopped more than once because the singer would not remain in her seat, plus she threw her shoes and cigarettes at various people who were roasting. Luckily, Courtney's antics landed her on news channels the next day, hence the event's enormous viewership. So, due to Courtney and her demons, awareness of me was heightened and my ticket sales increased more than I could have imagined. I am proud to say I partially owe my career to that crazy drunken bitch.

💜 When Courtney Love entered the makeup room, she asked the makeup artist to make her look like Marilyn Monroe. Seeing her on the roast, I think he thought she said "Marilyn Manson."

💜 Since I was closing the roast and Courtney was wreaking havoc throughout the night, I spent most of the time up on the dais writing a long list of Courtney Love put-downs, intending to shut her up if she were to pipe up and try to ruin my performance that evening. If you look closely at the roast's footage, you can see me furiously scribbling so that I would be armed and ready for Ms. Love. Ends up, all that effort was in vain. Courtney didn't utter a peep during my set other than laughter and, in fact, gave me a standing ovation and a huge kiss on the lips afterward. As a result of the kiss, I was high for five days.

❤ This roast was my first introduction to Andy Dick. Andy said he'd heard about me and kept grilling me before the roast and during the other performers' sets about what I was going to say about him. He asked me if I was going to say that he was gay, and he asked me if I was going to call him a child molester. I said no to both. I lied.

❤ Right before she went up to roast Pam, Sarah Silverman whispered something to Jimmy Kimmel. He immediately stood up, changed seats with someone, and held Courtney down, his arm firmly around her shoulder, throughout Sarah's entire set so the singer would not ruin his girlfriend's set. That, my friends, is true love.

❤ At one point, after a huge diatribe of unoriginal, unfunny stretched-out vagina jokes by a comic who did a mediocre job at best, I glanced at Pam Anderson to see if she was as shaken as I would have been. She was laughing but definitely phoning it in, and her feelings were clearly hurt due to the savage attack of this second-rate comedian. At the commercial break, as I watched, Tommy Lee stood up, went over to her, knelt in front of her, and asked her if she was okay.

She laughed it off, but having noted his concern and her sensitivity, I cut out all jokes from my roast that included the words "whore," "slut," and "vagina."

Jimmy Kimmel's Introduction

"On this channel on September tenth, our final roaster tonight has a one-woman show about divorce, dieting, and dating black people by choice, not because she has to because she is fat. It is called *I Would Rather Suck My Grandfather's Balls Than Watch It*. She is the reason Italian men beat their wives. Please welcome Lisa Lampanelli."

Worst Pun of the Evening

"Wait! What is your name? Lisa Lampa-Dykey." —Andy Dick

Best Rebuttal Joke About Me Ever by a Roastee

"Actually, Nick DiPaolo came up to me backstage and told me he was a huge Hole fan, so I introduced him to Lisa Lampanelli." —Pam Anderson

Favorite Joke About Me That Night

"Lisa Lampanelli is here . . . How does someone that looks like that make fun of Pam Anderson? That is like a turd making fun of a sunset." —David Spade

Favorite Joke of My Set

"Pam Anderson is a legend. She has dated Scott Baio, the singer from Poison, and the drummer from Mötley Crüe. Her life story should be a show on VH1 called *I Fucked the '80s*."

My Fake-Sincere Ending

"But all jokes aside, Pam, seriously, I would like to thank you for giving me the opportunity to make fun of you tonight. I think the reason the world loves you so much is that you are beautiful and famous, and you still treat everyone you meet with kindness and respect. As a woman not nearly as famous or as beautiful, let me say from the bottom of my heart: Knock it off, bitch! You're making me look like a foul-mouthed cunt!"

part two

How the Hell I
Turned Out This Way

CHAPTER FIVE

Macy's and Hamburger's

I am definitely not my mother's favorite. Check out the competition.

My brother is an executive at ESPN, has six kids from the same wife, has a big house in Connecticut, and coaches Little League. My sister is a high school teacher, has two kids from the same husband, has a big house in Connecticut, and volunteers with cripples and retards.

I, on the other hand, bang blacks, have a faggot for a best friend, and say "cunt" onstage for money. If my mother had to pull a *Sophie's Choice,* I know she'd pick me to be the one to go.

That is a joke I use in my act.

Of course, the crowd loves it and whoops and hollers whenever I describe myself. Sure—I sound super-cool to them. But let's face it: So many of them are gay, they clearly know the feelings of parental disapproval. However, up until recent years, before my parents gave me huge props for how I turned out as a career woman and as a person, I felt like I didn't measure up. I joke that when people ask my mom about me, she says, "Poor Lisa has been a little off since the accident."

"What accident?" they ask.

"Her conception."

But growing up, I couldn't help feeling that I fell short when compared with my sister, Nancy, and my brother, Len. And who could blame me? They were amazing, brilliant people—and my sister, well, she put the brown in "brown-noser."

In short, Nancy was perfect. At two years older than me, she was smart, but not in an "I'm smarter than you" way, friendly but not fake nice. In short, she was *exactly* like my mom. So when I came along and the role of family standout was already filled, I didn't know what to do with myself. Here I was the second kid, and my parents already had a good one, so what to do to get noticed? What to do? Perhaps I could make fun of colored people. That's always funny. No, actually I didn't stumble onto that until many chapters later.

Then I hit on it—I'd alternately misbehave and go off missing and pout. Then I'd be sure to get some carefully maneuvered middle-child-earned attention. At the time I didn't know this doesn't work well with parents, but it is amazingly effective with promoters and anyone else you are paying to make you happy.

One day when I was no older than three, I stomped up to my mother with a puss on. See, Nancy loved wearing dresses, complete with cute little patent-leather shoes and crinolines. She was the four-year-old Carrie Bradshaw of Trumbull, Connecticut. I, on the other hand, lived in pants and shorts. I glowered every time I had to put on my Sunday best, and one day on the way to church, I had had enough. Looking my mother square in the eye, I said, "Mommy, I'm mad at you."

Apparently, this was something she was used to from Little Lisa, because she responded, "What are you mad about *this time*?"

I screwed up my face and said, "I'm mad at you because you knowed I wanted to be a boy and you made me a girl," and clumped out of the room. (And no, this is not all leading up to me being a lesbian. Although if it did, it would give NPR's Terry Gross something meaty to latch on to in my *Fresh Air* interview.) When this impossible demand didn't yield the result I wanted (what was my mom supposed to do? Twitch her nose and have me sprout nuts and a penis? The only documented incident of that happening spawned Clay Aiken), I trudged outside with my only friend in the world, Teddy, my uniquely named teddy bear. Even back then, I was big into stereotypes.

"That's right, Teddy," I spoke loudly to the disheveled toy. "Nobody loves us. All we have is each other." And then I added, "If you ever leave me, I will kill you!" Now that I think about it, the only difference between that and my relationships now is that, as I have grown up, I have replaced teddy bears with chubby gay men. So I guess I'm still hanging with bears.

Of course, ever the attention whore, I spoke these plaintive words just within earshot of my sister, who I knew would run and tell my mother—she told her *everything*. I waited in the driveway for my mother to come rushing out, gather me in her arms *Father Knows Best*–style, and reassure me that yes, indeed, someone besides Teddy had my back.

But remember: This was the Lampanelli family, and things didn't always go the way I'd planned.

Oh, don't get me wrong, my sister spread the word to my mom, but instead of getting the desired result, what I got instead was a swat on the butt and a dust rag. That was the day I learned that playing the victim didn't get me love and affection—it got me a sore ass and a roomful of furniture to polish. Needless to say, that wasn't the last time my ass got sore in the hopes that someone would say they loved me.

While my sister and I have a great relationship now, it wasn't always that way. Ever the tattletale, she lived for the chance to get dirt on me and spread it to the powers that be. Of course, as the two girls of the family, we shared a bedroom on the second floor of my family's colonial-style house. One night when I was around ten years old, I went to bed still infuriated at my sister about some disagreement or another we'd had during the daylight hours. My mother turned out the lights, and I lay there in the twin bed across the room from my sister, continuing the silent treatment I had begun giving her hours before. By the way, the silent treatment doesn't work that well in bed and in the dark. The other person just assumes you're asleep.

Glaring at her in the dark, I heard something. "Good night, Lisa," she said in the same faux-sweet, singsong voice perfected by Nellie Oleson in *Little House on the Prairie* after the show jumped the shark. I ignored her and scowled at her even harder. "Good *night*, Lisa," she repeated, this time with more bite and an audible edge. When again she was met with my stony silence, she upped her ante.

"*I. Love. You!!*" she said, biting off every syllable, each word dripping with sarcasm.

I stuck to my resolve. I wouldn't say "good night" and I *certainly* wouldn't tell that bitch I loved her. She had to be fucking kidding! I haven't said that back to men who were fondling my ass at the time—I definitely wasn't telling it to her.

The next thing I heard can only be described as shrieking as she forced the manufactured crocodile tears down her pudgy, pouty little face. "*Mmmmooooommmmyyyyy!* I told Lisa I loved her and she wouldn't say it back!" What is this, our honeymoon? I'm trying to sleep, bitch!

My mom stormed into the room and—you guessed it—that bought me another sore bottom and some heavy-duty banister polishing (and I don't mean that in the biblical sense).

While my sister craved my mother's approval and sought it in the typical oldest-child ways—excelling and trying hard in school, asking her advice, and generally being a mirror image of her—as I got older, I devised other ways. I learned early on that if I wanted to outshine my sister, I had to do it in a big way. Now, when you're a kid, any attention is good attention, so I went to town. Since my sister was already an expert eater, I pretended to like food that no one else would eat—just to heighten my parents' awareness that I was an individual.

(This wasn't the last time I put things in my mouth that no one else would for love and attention.)

I asked my mother to buy limes and lemons, and when she brought them home each Saturday morning with the week's shopping, I would peel them and eat them whole. I reveled in the interest I was paid as I choked down the sour fruit, stopping only to look up to make sure people were watching. I did the same with sticks of butter, bowls of grated cheese, and entire cans of black olives. Eating to get attention is a behavior that I continued into my high school days. Feeling ignored in comparison to beautiful girls in class like the Sophia Loren of our school, Donna Rago, I would eat entire Swiss Rolls (the enormous version of Yodels) in one bite, an action that got me lots of laughs but very few gentleman callers. Oral wasn't as popular back then as it is now.

If my sister was the queen mother of us kids and I was the jester, from the moment my brother, Len, was born, he was the king. His nickname from birth was even "King of the Hill," and we just loved him. In short, Leonard was *adorable*— blond, giggly, chubby—and my sister and I couldn't spoil him enough. And why shouldn't we have? He was cuter than us, and he added a huge sense of fun to the family. One of my earliest memories of my brother was when he was six and insisted my mother play the 45 of "Cecilia" by Simon and Garfunkel over and over. It probably would have been even cuter if he hadn't been dry-humping my Raggedy Ann doll on the couch at the time, but still . . .

Of course, we all loved the song—we had a cousin and a great-aunt named Cecilia, so the tune was beloved by everyone, especially my mother. You can't imagine her look of shock when my brother—just a mere first-grader—belted out the words "making love in the afternoon" in front of company.

Of course, my brother had no idea what he was saying but loved the fact that my mother turned bright red, my father squirmed uncomfortably, and my sister and I erupted in peals of laughter. My brother proved long before I did that the Lampanellis don't work clean.

My brother wasn't the only one who loved to get laughs. As early as I can remember, I relished being the comic relief of the family. For some reason, I could make my mother laugh in times of tension—and sometimes the things I said or did to get laughs would have gotten my brother or sister in heaps of trouble. But since my role in the family seemed to be the funny one, I got away with it unscathed.

The first laugh I remember getting came with a valuable lesson in when to stop. My family was having dinner at the home of my father's favorite aunt, Aunt Rose, and her husband, Uncle Dom, who was also our oil deliveryman. Just a quick aside: Going to an Italian family function is like pulling up to Home Depot. Everybody there knows someone who can fix your car, paint your house, or unclog your drain. We Italians may not have many doctors in our families, but we do have a lot of plumbers—probably due to our huge amount of body hair.

Anyway, I was about eight at the time, and it was around Thanksgiving. As we ate, I said that someday I would love to go to the famous parade at Macy's and Bamberger's. (That was what the store was called before Macy's dropped the second name, presumably in an attempt to make the store sound less Jew-y.)

Now, remember, at the time I was a mere tot. So I unwittingly said, "I want to go to the parade at Macy's and *Ham-burger's*." Well, that's all it took for the table to explode in what can only be described as guffaws. And believe me, from the second I heard that laughter, I was hooked. I can honestly say that was the exact moment I decided to become a comedian, even though it took me the next twenty-two years to summon up the guts to try.

However, being the attention hound I am and an extremist by nature, one laugh wasn't enough. As the laughter at the table died down, ol' Shecky Lampanelli went for a twofer: "Yeah, Macy's and Hamburger's!" I repeated. As if in slow motion, each family member turned to me and stared, their smiles gone. Note to self: Never try to milk the joke—even when you're eight. Coincidentally, years later, my famous "Macy's and Hamburger's" line is Carrot Top's big closer.

Being Italian meant that meals were, of course, the thing around which our family's life revolved. Relatives were always coming over for a big dinner, or we were always eating over at relatives' homes. As is common knowledge, eating is the most important thing in any Italian's life. We Italians learn from a very early age to eat until you're sick. If you don't, you're dishonoring the memory of somebody back in Italy who died of starvation three generations ago.

As a result, Italian families are huge—literally and figuratively. Everybody is named after one another so there's a Big Mike and a Little Mike, even though they both weigh over three hundred pounds. Italians are also fat because everyone's nonna, or grandmother, makes the best sauce, and our family was no different: The family sauce appeared at every gathering, even on Thanksgiving. Our menu: turkey and lasagna. In fact, in our house, by the time we got to the sixth—and main—course (the turkey, stuffing, and vegetables), no one was hungry anymore, and the bird went untouched. Untouched, that is, except for the pile of turkey skin I consumed to get some attention. By the way, even then I preferred the dark meat.

But food was the only thing my family overindulged in. We all may have been fat, but there wasn't a drug addict or so much as a drunk in the bunch. That's because my mom scared us straight. Growing up in the seventies, we had no shortage of antidrug programs, a direct result of the sixties' free love and pot boom. However, being children of the forties and fifties, my parents had never consumed anything stronger than Communion wine, and my mother was going to see to it that we didn't either.

I remember early on my mother telling us not to "smoke anything that is grass or looks like it," and, to our horror, she told us she'd read that anyone who "drank acid" (her version of "took acid") would go so insane that they would take nail files, stick them behind their eyes, and pop their eyeballs out onto the table. Of course, she could have scared us more with the real dangers of drugs, the biggest of which was that you might someday become a sixty-year-old hippie. Parents, if you want your kids to say no to drugs, just have them hang out with a stinky middle-aged woman who's bartering organic herbs for a massage.

However, as a child, bloody eyeballs on a table is a pretty scary image, and I don't know about my brother and sister, but it worked for me. I have never tried anything stronger than pot, and the few times I did, I became even more intensely paranoid than I am when I'm straight. Even drinking held little charm for me. I'm not sure if it's how uncomfortable I am with being out of control or the fact that I have the world's worst hangovers, but whichever it is, my only drug of choice has been food—and, of course, men. And in recent years, both happened to be chocolate.

My mother's scary stories weren't just about the dangers of drugs and alcohol. She was fiercely determined we not talk to strangers, 'cause you know where that can lead. When either my sister or I was in a public bathroom, my mother would be hovering directly outside the stall, watching like a hawk to make sure nobody so much as asked us for a square of toilet paper. My brother, on the other hand, presented a different problem. He was a boy and needed to pee in the men's room, and my mom certainly wasn't going in there with him.

One day, I saw my brother race into the men's room and beat it right back to the car in what can only be described as a flash. When I asked him why he was in such a hurry, he told me that my mother had told him she'd read a story in the paper about a man who had accosted a young boy in a public restroom and cut his wee-wee off. I couldn't get that visual out of my head. When I asked my mother what the boy was left with, she said matter-of-factly, "A hole," and continued her reading. Today, moms use the same story, only they usually show Andy Dick's mugshot when they're telling it.

Now, I don't know if that "news story" was real or simply my mom's attempt at a scare tactic, but I can tell you that it worked. I'm assuming my brother still has all his genitalia (he has six children, so you do the math), and none of us has ever been kidnapped or molested. I like to think that's because of my mom's protectiveness and not because we weren't attractive or desirable enough.

Obviously, Gloria's been a colorful mom, to say the least, but we always had room in our hearts for my dad, Len. Off to work he went every day to a job that was too complicated or boring for me to even now know what it was, and whenever he disappeared for a few days on a business trip, he came back loaded with gifts. My first pair of bell-bottom pants was from a trip he took to L.A., and I still have the matchbooks and other little trinkets he took from the Hiltons and Marriotts where Sikorsky Aircraft had him stay. I love the towels, pillows, and iron to this day. And the hangers with actual hooks on them! Priceless!

While my dad's gifts were fun and at the time seemed exotic, it was my mother who bought me my most memorable gift of all. One year, she presented us all with cemetery plots so that we could be buried together as a family. She knew what a hassle it would be for us to scramble to buy her and my father plots if they should meet an untimely demise, so she grabbed two for them and, while she was at it, had the cemetery guy throw in six for us kids and our potential spouses. If I never get married, I get to use the extra plot to bury my shoes . . . or my guilt.

As I finish writing this, I'm about to check out of the sumptuous Peabody hotel in Memphis, and I'm inspecting the room for stuff my folks might like. My dad never has enough shoehorns, so I take that. My mom needs travel shampoo for going up to their house at Cape Cod. Lastly, I grab them both ivory-colored Peabody pens since whenever I call the house it takes them about three hours to find something to write with. I know I'll take these things to them in Connecticut, and they'll make a fuss over them as if they're real gifts.

And, unlike funeral plots, they can use them while they're still alive.

CHAPTER SIX

Sit, Kneel, Stand

I n any twelve-step program—Alcoholics Anonymous, Narcotics Anonymous, Eating Disorders Anonymous, all the way down the food chain to Rageaholics Anonymous—there is a saying you hear at least once at each and every gathering: "Ninety meetings in ninety days." Apparently, that's the number of meetings someone in early sobriety needs to attend for the twelve-stepping to really kick in and for him to surrender to his Higher Power.

Well, if you grew up in the Lampanelli house in 1972, there was a slightly different version of "Ninety in ninety."

It was "Forty in forty," as in "Forty Masses in forty days," or as I used to call it, "Priest-a-Palooza."

Those forty days make up the most dreaded time period in any Catholic's year: Lent. While other children my age were thrilled to usher out the winter months and dive straight into spring, I looked at the approach of the new season with a mixture of anxiety, trepidation, and near terror. For the forty days of Lent, which began with Ash Wednesday (a day so evil it ends Mardi Gras), we would be attending Mass *every single day* until Jesus moved the stone out of the way and pulled his Houdini act. *Forty freakin' Masses in forty days!* Frankly, I'd get burned out going to forty movies in forty days, and movie theaters have cushioned seats and better snacks. But it was 1972, I was only eleven, and at that time, my mother, Gloria, was my Higher Power.

Growing up Catholic isn't easy. I'm sure there are tougher religions out there that require stricter adherence to tradition and, from what I understand, involve things like fasting (great idea, Jews! Celebrate by getting together and *starving*!) or the stoning of whores, which, by the way, means killing them, not what Led Zeppelin used to do backstage. Sadly, I cannot report on these other religions because I am content to stay ignorant about other cultures and peoples. My logic has always been: What I don't know can't hurt me—unless it involves a terror threat or a rash on someone's nut sack. But me? I grew up Catholic—not "go to Mass on Easter and Christmas to show off our new clothes" Catholic, but real hard-core, "one step away from making a movie about the crucifixion, then getting drunk and badmouthing the Jews in Hollywood" Catholic.

As early as I can remember, my mom went to church *a lot*.

Not just every Sunday like my father and the rest of us. No! Gloria went to Mass *every day,* which, quite honestly, put a lot of pressure on the priest to keep coming up with new shit. I remember her leaving the house at 7:55 A.M. before work each morning—apparently the first Mass of the day was half-price, just like L.A. movie theaters—or at 4:55 P.M. (sometimes both, depending how insane we drove her) to catch eight o'clock or five o'clock Mass at Trumbull's horrendously named Most Precious Blood Church, which stood horrendously close to our house. I remember wondering why she was so into church. All that praying didn't really seem to do much good—she and my dad were stuck in the same argument-filled marriage; my brother, sister, and I engaged in behavior that ranged from downright awful to barely squeaking by; and they made the same money, lived in the same house, and still drove a Valiant and an LTD. You'd figure that amount of praying would have at least gotten us a second phone extension and a time-share in Boca. Then again, thank God she went to church a lot. If she needed that much prayer to stay just inside the bounds of sanity, imagine if she didn't pray at all. I wouldn't have made it past the age of eight.

All in all, my mom going to church that much didn't bother me. It bought us an extra hour each day to gang up on my sister, and to make prank phone calls (this was in the days before caller ID ruined this hilarious activity). But it wasn't all wine and roses. All that time my mom was away in the evenings meant a lot more half-assed dinners. As a kid, I ate more weenies than a gay prostitute.

As a good Catholic, my mother loved Lent, and she often spoke about it in our house with reverence. For those of you who aren't Catholic, I will explain. Lent starts on Ash Wednesday, which is a day you can't wear a nice outfit because you have to go to church and have the priest put ashes on your head, your clothes, and inside your car. Its only purpose is to mark you so people know you're not a Jew in case there's a hostage situation. The ashes are ground up and kept in a bowl. So if a Catholic man ever tries to put his cigarette out on your forehead, he's not a priest. He's just being a dick.

All during Lent, you're supposed to give up something you love as a sacrifice to God. I guess Catholics figured if Jesus could come down to earth, hang with us mortals for thirty-three years, and then die for our sins, the least we could do is give up chocolate. (To this day, I still feel guilty banging black guys during the month of April.) And that's what most of us did—we gave up something—but as most religious people do, we had ulterior motives. I remember one year giving up dessert (of course, this was in early puberty and I thought forty days without cake would help me lose a good ten pounds off my newly expanding figure), and one year, I gave up lunch altogether. The fact that I more than made up for the skipped meal at dinner was something between me and my maker. Looking back, I don't know who I was trying to impress— God, Jenny Craig, or the cute guy who sat behind me in science class.

I always found it somewhat odd that people "sacrificed" their asses off when it came to food all throughout Lent, and then when Easter finally got here, we gorged on chocolate bunnies and Cadbury eggs. But, as all good Catholics know, nothing says "Thank you for dying for our sins" like a Snickers bar shaped like an crucifix. Looking back, I guess it's easy to see why Muslims hate us. They have jihads and suicide bombers. We have a guy dressed up like a rabbit and hide colored eggs.

But in our house, Lent wasn't just a time to forfeit plea-sure—it was "the cure." Every chance she got, my mother reminded us that one year early in their marriage, my father had given up smoking for Lent and had never picked up a cigarette again. This inspired my mom, and every Lent she gave up one of her vices—food, food, or food—and encour-aged us to do the same. It all felt harmless enough—what's the worst that could happen? We drop a few pounds and God loves us more. To me, that was win-win. Each Lent, we gave up something we liked (I was never committed enough to giving up something I *loved*—c'mon, I'm not a fanatic), we logged in our hour a week in church every Sunday, and my daily-Mass mom left us a blissful, stress-free hour each day.

That is, until 1972, when things took an unexpected twist, and I would never look at church the same way again.

I was eleven and was at that awkward stage where I felt like neither a boy nor a girl, and I liked it that way. Some people never get over that—David Bowie and Prince both spring to mind. I studied, I fantasized about kissing nonthreatening powder-puff rockers like Bobby Sherman and David Cassidy, and I cried at the end of *Black Beauty*. Today, I still cry at the end of black beauty, but now it's in reference to a penis. I was just rolling through life, keeping my nose clean, and suddenly, the edict came down: All three of us kids would have to attend church with my mother for all forty days of Lent every single night at five o'clock. I had never loved church in the first place, always feeling embarrassed at the way my mom and my sister sang just a little too loud during the hymns, dreading the moment one of them would toss in a prayer "for the safety and health of our families" during the part where you were allowed to pray out loud (fuckin' show-offs!). Church had always been a chore, but now that we had to do our "forty in forty," church became a punishment, like Chinese water torture or sitting through anything that stars Steven Seagal.

As Lent came to a close that year, I was more than a little relieved. I endured Holy Thursday Mass, which was a little more tolerable 'cause, as a more special Mass than those ordinary, dreary daily ones, it was a prime people-watching opportunity. Holy Thursday is the warm-up Mass for Easter; in fact, the congregation's clothes became nicer and their hair grew higher as the big day approached. After Holy Thursday, we geared up for Good Friday. For those of you who don't know, Good Friday is the most ill-named holy day in the Roman Catholic religion. It is the day that Jesus died on the cross, so when you think about it, it really wasn't a very good Friday for Jesus. Good Friday in our house was the day that we had to sit in silence—that's right, no TV, no playing, no nothin'—from noon to three P.M. because, according to authorities, those were precisely the three hours that Jesus died on the cross. Fun stuff, huh? Now I know how people must feel when they see Tracy Morgan perform live.

The absolute worst thing about Good Friday was a torture ritual known as the Stations of the Cross, a bizarre routine where you sit, kneel, stand, and circle the inside of the church to replicate the hell Jesus suffered during his last few hours on earth. In short, it's aerobics for the devout. Up, down, up, down—the Stations of the Cross are so boring, it's like doing the StairMaster without your iPod. To make matters worse, they blow incense in your face—not the kind you burn so your parents don't smell pot, the kind they burn to kill the smell of rotting corpses.

Luckily, the day wasn't all doom and gloom—on Good Friday we were rewarded for our sorrow with a trip to McDonald's for the Catholic-friendly choice on the menu, the Filet-O-Fish, since the "No meat on Fridays" rule was especially important during Lent. And does McDonald's ever cash in with the Catholics during Lent! I remember one year I ate so many Lenten Happy Meals, I collected a Pontius Pilate action figure and seven of the twelve apostles.

Possibly due to our bitching, whining, and moaning, my mother let the "forty Masses in forty days" go the next Lent. In '73, she had a better idea. In some kind of weird outreach program, churches started offering Masses in the home. Of course, after the movie *The Exorcist,* most people stopped having priests over. But not my mom! She figured why drive those excruciating five minutes up the street to Most Precious Blood—finally and mercifully renamed Christ the King Church, thereby nominally reducing its creep factor—when you could invite a priest into your home, practice your best manners, and serve him ziti afterward? Guess who's coming to dinner? No, not Sidney Poitier, motherfuckers! It's Father Doro.

As priests go, Father Doro was pretty cool. An old guy of around thirty-five—when you're twelve, everybody seems "old"—he said a rather uneventful Mass at our house for our immediate family. The Mass was in the evening, thank God, because the usual pressure to stay awake during the service was on in full force. Nobody noticed when you nodded off at Sunday Mass when you were surrounded by three hundred people, but when you're one of five, you better keep your eyes open or a beat-down is comin' your way.

A little later that year, puberty was in full swing for me, and *everything* was hot. When you come from a repressed Catholic family, sex seems to pop up everywhere, and nowhere was it more present than at church. I had always found Jesus pretty attractive—his muscle tone was beyond reproach and he *had* died for my sins (that's commitment)—but now hotness in church came in the form of a visiting Latino priest, Father Guilliani, and he was *muy caliente,* indeed.

I first noticed Father Guilliani when I joined the folk group at Christ the King. Always craving attention and having figured out the three guitar chords every good song was made up of—C, F, and G—I signed up to practice twice a week and play at ten o'clock Mass every Sunday. From the folk group's spot on the altar—three steps above the congregation—I could scan the crowd for cute guys, have a clear view of the hot Jesus statue, and gawk at Padre El Guapo. Since our folk group was allowed to play "cool" music, I serenaded the visiting priest with renditions of "Both Sides Now" and "The Impossible Dream," imagining that he would follow his impossible dream of leaving the priesthood and running away *Thorn Birds*–style with a twelve-year-old former tomboy.

Looking back, I think this fantasy made my penchant for black men a natural transition. Dating a black guy is a lot like dating a priest—they're forbidden, they don't want kids, and if your family catches you banging one, they kick you out. I was snapped back to reality one day when my mother casually mentioned that Father Guilliani was no more. Alas, he was going back to his native Guatemala, Panama, or whatever Third World country he hailed from to help the financially bankrupt people of South America instead of the spiritually bankrupt middle-class folks of Trumbull, Connecticut. Either that or he was offered a job saying prayers at the beginning of the cockfights. I forget which.

Things had really changed for me since my days of playing nun with my sister in our backyard when we were six and eight. I had gone from wearing one of my brother's cloth diapers on my head and pretending to take Communion with a most pious look and heavy-lidded eyes to bawling over a departed man of God whom I could never have. But by then, there was no turning back. As my mother made a small sign of the cross on her forehead every time we passed a church, I crossed my fingers that another piece of eye candy like Father Guilliani would make his way to us. But no matter how many times I listened to "If" by Bread, my prayers went unanswered and another paunchy Irish priest with a gin-blossomed nose took his place. It is not surprising that I eventually lost faith.

Church became something to avoid, and the minute I turned sixteen, I was licensed to skip. My partner in crime was my little brother, Leonard, who by thirteen was cooler than I'll ever be. Our church became the video game arcade of the Trumbull Shopping Park—also ironically five minutes from our suburban home. The church and the arcade each five minutes away! There might as well have been an angel and devil on my shoulders. Every Sunday, my brother and I would jump into my grandfather's old Plymouth Duster, look at each other, and say, "So, where're we going?" and off we'd go to spend fifty minutes with Ms. Pac-Man, Asteroids, and Moon Patrol. With a quick stop at church to pick up a weekly bulletin—written proof that we'd been there—we'd get home just in time to spend the day with the family, silently praying that no one would ask us, "So, how was the sermon?" Luckily, at that age, kids are known to be sullen and shrug a lot, so whenever the question came up, we got through it by grunting and, if all else failed, storming upstairs and slamming the door. And if my folks pushed for an answer, I could always say, "I don't remember because someone ripped one and I couldn't stop laughing," which no one would question because there is nothing funnier than a fart vibrating off a wooden pew during the homily.

Once I went off to college, church became a moot point. Since all my life my mother had served as our alarm clock— providing us with some rude awakenings—I'd lay awake every Sunday morning and watch the minutes tick by, waiting for her to rustle me up for that morning's service. The first week I came home from college, there was no knock at my door. As the departure time for the family approached, I was still "sleeping" and no one had made an attempt to rouse me. As the door quietly shut behind the rest of the family, I realized that I had won the fight. My mother had given up—she would no longer struggle to get a scowling, sulky teenager to Sunday Mass. A slight feeling of being left behind washed over me and for a moment, I felt totally alone.

Hallelujah! My prayers had been answered!

Oh, c'mon—it's not like they weren't coming back.

In the thirty years since then, I have only attended church

a handful of times—once to get married, a half-dozen times to see people get married, and a few times to participate in confirmations, baptisms, funerals, and other rituals. I have proudly held my nephew Luke and my niece Eve, serving as their godmother, which gives me the written, church-sanctioned permission to spoil them for the rest of their lives. Also, in those thirty years, I have only dined with one other priest, Father John, the priest who performed my marriage and my nephew's baptism and was later dismissed because of his, ahem, infidelities. I like to think that Father John is happier now that he's out of the priesthood, and I have to think that while he was eating with us, he was entertaining only the purest of thoughts. Hey, I can dream too.

Oh, and Father Guilliani, on the off chance that you're reading this and have left the priesthood, give a bitch a call. I think the two of us could have uno goodo tiempo, Papi!

CHAPTER SEVEN

School Daze,

or I'll Have an Honor Roll with Extra Jelly, Please

very class has a fat, smelly kid who eats paper, paste, and boogers. In my class, that kid's name was Dominic.

Dominic is always blamed if there's a fart smell in the room. Dominic always looks a little dirty. And he usually has dandruff, zits, and greasy hair—and sometimes all of that's in his ears.

Oh, and one more thing: Dominic is the kid you never, *ever* want to sit next to in class. 'Cause in Catholic school, seating assignments are for *life*—or at least what feels like life, an entire school year. Sitting next to Dominic is the grammar school equivalent of being stuck next to the fat guy on an air-plane for almost ten months—only worse, because you can't pretend to be asleep.

Fourth grade was the grade my luck ran out. I sailed through my first three years at Most Precious Blood grammar school with no problems that I can remember. In fact, I floated through my first few grades in a state that can only be called delusional. I liked everyone, everyone liked me, and I thought it would stay that way forever. Then came Ms. Haas's fourth-grade class and my seating assignment next to Dominic.

"Offer it up as a sacrifice," said Ms. Haas.

That was every Catholic school teacher's stock answer: "Offer it up as a sacrifice."

Don't like playing kickball in gym class? Offer it up as a sacrifice. Don't like having religion class every single day? Of-fer it up as a sacrifice. And don't like your seating assignment next to Mr. Stink for the entire year? You better damn sure offer it up as a sacrifice—and hold your freakin' nose. Every time I heard those six infuriating words, I felt like scream-ing, "Hey, Sister, if my parents really wanted me to sacrifice, they would've sent me to public school." I mean, here we were shelling out big bucks for this bullshit—so I figured they either owed me a new seat or Ol' Smelly a bar of soap.

Soon after entering the classroom that September, I dis-covered the entire year would be one big sacrifice. But un-like the typical sacrificial lamb, I had a little something in me that said, "We're not gonna take it," long before Twisted Sister was a twinkle in Dee Snider's mascara-lined eye. I may have been a scrawny nine-year-old with crooked teeth and even crooked-er bangs, but I wasn't about to lie down and accept it. Like my grandpa in the nursing home used to say to the nurses, "Hey, bitch, if I wanted to smell shit all day, I wouldn't be paying you to change my Depends."

After being shut down by Ms. Haas when I tried to plead my case for a new seat assignment, I silently decided that she was the enemy. This bitch couldn't be trusted. One of the few teachers at the school who wasn't a nun, Ms. Haas was a rebel in her own right—she wore *pants*—but her rebellion benefitted only her. She lounged at the front of the classroom, her chubby legs and cankles extended under her desk, her arms folded behind her head, elbows akimbo, while we sat with hands folded and ankles crossed under our desks in uncomfortable, poly-blend, plaid sandpaper uniforms. We stared in disbelief, our mouths watering, as she cracked open one of the many boxes of Girl Scout cookies she kept in her desk—cookies that she devoured one at a time as we licked our chops and tried to calculate how much longer it was until lunchtime.

And what I would have given for that kind of lunch—a lunch of Thin Mints, Do-Si-Dos, Tagalongs, and Trefoils! But no, my mother had different ideas when it came to nutrition, and they were a source of misery and embarrassment on a daily basis, which coincidentally is the theme of the entire Catholic school system.

Let me explain: To this day, I love a nice bologna sandwich. Yep, a bologna sandwich—and not just to attract the black men either. If you asked me what would be my perfect food day, it would consist of a bowl of Cheerios for breakfast, a bologna sandwich—on Wonderbread, of course—for lunch, and a Swanson's fried chicken TV dinner for supper. "Why such bland, processed food?" you might ask. 'Cause as any amateur shrink will tell you, you always crave what you never got in childhood. And what I got in my lunch bag at school was anything but bland, anything but bologna.

For example, there were the stuffed pepper sandwiches. Yep—as if stuffed peppers weren't fatty, greasy, and smelly enough the night before for dinner, my mom figured we'd love 'em the second time around at lunch. Now, it's one thing to eat stuffed peppers when they're hot. It's quite another to eat them when they're slimy enough to make a frat boy puke. On a weekly basis, my mother would wedge this dinnertime "treat" between two slices of thin white bread that were hardly a barrier to their seeping, oily goodness. By the time lunchtime arrived, my sandwich would be a wet, soppy mess, and the brown paper bag was nearly see-through, the shiny, slippery mass a beacon that screamed, "I'm Italian! I'm different! No wonder I sit next to smelly Dominic!" In a grade where fitting in is everything, I stood out, and I wasn't happy about it.

And speaking of which, yes, I was stuck with a brown paper bag. I didn't even get a cool lunch pail—like one with the Fonz on it. I had a ratty old bag, although for almost two weeks, I convinced people it was a *Sanford and Son* lunch box.

Needless to say, with my lunches, there were no trades from my classmates. Trust me—nobody wants to swap their raisins or cupcakes for a stuffed pepper sandwich. The only thing I ever got in exchange for one of my mom's meals was a "Yeah, right, bitch!" You know how sometimes mothers send little messages in the lunches they pack? My friends' moms' messages were things like "I love you." The message I got was "Your father doesn't like leftovers."

Fourth grade was also the first time I remember standing up to authority, the one theme that has been constant throughout the rest of my life.

My first opportunity to look the higher-ups straight in the eye and flip them off came in the form of my little brother, Leonard, who had started first grade that year. He was my pride and joy—I thought he was adorable and perfect—and when I found out he was cast to play the lead in his class production of *Casper, the Friendly Ghost,* I couldn't wait until the day of the show. As Halloween approached, I grew more and more excited to show off my little brother—after all, I knew him when he was *nobody*—and witness him in the starring role.

Well, one thing or another happened in class that day, and Ms. Haas threatened our unruly class: "Keep misbehaving and you won't be allowed to attend the school play today." My head shot up from the penis I was doodling in a school library book. If this bitch wanted my attention, she had it! In my first ever "Do you have any idea who I am?" moment, I asked to go to the girls' room and marched directly across the hall into the principal's office instead. This was my first recollection of ever going over somebody's head, and I remember it felt great!

"My brother is the star of that show, and *I'm going*!" I told Sister Catherine, our principal. Rightfully taken aback, Sister stared at me in disbelief. "Ms. Haas is saying we can't go to the show, and I'm going. If she won't change her mind, I'm calling my mom." Whether she was impressed by my ballsy attitude, afraid of the famous Lampanelli temper, or just wanted to get the smell of old stuffed pepper sandwich out of her office, Sister Catherine did the job and told Ms. Haas that yes, indeed, our grade would be attending the performance. I beamed happily from a pew in the church-cum-auditorium as my brother made his entrance covered in a sheet and said his lines, "Booo" and "Oooo," in the right order. I wouldn't have missed it for the world. It would have been perfect if I didn't have to sit next to that smelly ass Dominic.

❖

There are two schools of thought when it comes to high school. Either it is the best time of your life or the worst time of your life. My high school experience, however, was somewhere in between. My high school years were consumed with boys, tennis team, drama club, and a relationship captured perfectly in *Romy and Michele's High School Reunion.*

Like Romy and Michele, I thought I was having a blast. I thought everyone liked me. And I thought there were no cooler people in the school than me and my best friend. Only instead of palling around with another girl, my Romy came in the form of a boy: Jimmy Pantelones.

Jimmy absolutely defied category. I had never met anyone like him before. A mischievous, short, sexually ambiguous guy who seemed to be balding from the age of ten—and by the way, if you're reading this, Jimmy, I mean that in the most complimentary of ways—Jimmy was smart but cool, rich but relatable, studious but dabbled in pot. (And by the way, if Jimmy's kids are reading this, by "pot," I mean . . . oh, fuck it! That bald hermaphrodite couldn't possibly have any kids!) In short, the guy was beyond description. And we were inseparable for four solid years.

Jimmy and I used to joke that people invited us to parties as the entertainment. I'm not sure about that, but I do remember laughing nonstop—and believe it or not, it had nothing to do with pot. I met Jimmy when my first six years of grammar school at Most Precious Blood ended and three local Catholic schools merged for the seventh and eighth grades as Trumbull Catholic Regional School. There, I was exposed to kids from St. Catherine's School and St. Teresa's School—kids the likes of which I had never met before. They were all white, Catholic, middle-class . . . well, at the time, they seemed different.

There were Roxanne and Patrice, two edgy girls who wore sparkle knee socks and David Bowie haircuts with their school uniforms. God, were they cool! But they were nice too. There were even rumors that Roxanne, who was at least a B-cup at twelve years old, smoked cigarettes, something that my pre-period, flat-as-a-board self could hardly imagine. There were Kim Horvath and John Spiegel, two blond lookalikes who were "going out." Of course, "going out" didn't mean they went on dates. "Going out" back then pretty much consisted of them walking hand-in-hand to class, slow-dancing at our eighth-grade dance, and generally making the rest of us girls feel inadequate for not having a boyfriend. But still, it seemed so rad! I mean, a couple? In seventh grade? At Most Precious Blood, the closest I got to boys was during games of touch football, where me and Patty Kraull (an exact duplicate of Peppermint Patty, in looks and probably sexuality) would sack the quarterback and then celebrate by dry-humping him until the coach pulled us off. In short, my world expanded the minute I left MPB behind, and Jimmy Pantelones was my key to a whole new way of life.

Grammar school had been, to put it mildly, a very sheltered experience for me. Sure, I had learned to stick up for myself, but I had still kept relatively to myself. Well, Jimmy changed all that. He was hilarious, he had a tennis court *and* a swimming pool in the backyard, his mother and sisters were fashionable and skinny, and his father was a doctor—an ob-gyn. Best of all, they were friendly and happy and joked around a lot. I loved going to the house for dinner—the absence of drama and chaos was a welcome change. And the fact that Jimmy and I loved making out in their music room—I mean, how rich do you have to be to have a music room?—only added to the draw of the place. In my house, the "music room" was a room where you turned up the music so you didn't have to hear all the screaming and yelling.

Kim Horvath and John Spiegel may have been the class couple in middle school, but Jimmy and I, in my opinion, were the *best* couple. I mean, who wants to hang around with Donny and Marie when you can have Cheech and Chong? We had fun together, we listened to the best music (Yes, Jethro Tull, Gentle Giant), and we watched the coolest TV shows and laughed our asses off. And we were a lethal team when it came to the classroom—both of us were smart as a whip and not afraid to use our wits for evil.

Of course, Trumbull Catholic Regional was still Catholic school and everything was a privilege—even getting a drink of water from the fountain, especially in the sweltering month of June before school let out. And during the June we were to graduate, the members of my eighth-grade class had spirits that were running high, with short attention spans to match.

As the days went by, I got ballsier. And Ms. S, our social

studies teacher, got the brunt of my bad behavior. Why? She was the gazelle with the broken foot—and her little frail teacher frame and demeanor begged me to push her to the limit. Plus, she was one of those teachers who felt that students would respond if you treated them with respect and dignity. That's the biggest fallacy since "A man will respect you in the morning." Puleeze!

In a particularly gutsy move—one that makes me nervous thinking about it today—I was turned completely around talking to Jimmy and our friend Monica O'Neil *during a lecture.* I don't mean looking over my shoulder—I mean completely facing the desk in back of me from my seat in the front row, blatantly ignoring Ms. S's words. As she stammered to keep our attention, she whipped out the big guns: "Lisa, if you do not turn around immediately, you will prevent your entire row from getting a drink of water."

For most of the students in the class, that would be their call to order. But not for me, Little Miss Can't Be Wrong. Ever so sweetly, I turned around, looked Ms. S right in the eye, and said, "That's okay, Ms. S. I'm not thirsty." Without missing a beat, I turned around again and queried, "What about you, Monica, are *you* thirsty?"

"No, not particularly, Lisa. What about you, Jimmy?" came her reply.

"No, I'm fine. Wet as a whistle."

Now, if anyone ever did that to me at one of my shows, I would fingerbang their asshole with the microphone. But back then, the dumbstruck Ms. S just sputtered her way through the rest of the lecture and gave up.

Over the summer, we heard the news that Ms. S had quit

her job because, rumor had it, she had had a nervous breakdown. I would be lying if I said I didn't feel just a little bit proud of myself. When you're an adult, it's easy to ruin someone's life. But when you can do it as a kid—that's a gift.

But the Jimmy and Lisa story hit a bump in the road after graduation, something that made me think the relationship was as doomed as doomed could be.

I spent most of the summer between eighth grade and freshman year of high school at the tennis courts at Trumbull High School, and it was there that I met the guy for whom I risked everything: Dave Cloutier (no, not the douchebag from *Full House*—a different Dave). Dave was the number-one tennis seed in his age category in the entire town and I thought he was hot. Now that I look back on it, he had goofy, round Coke-bottle glasses and bowed legs, but I thought he was the shit. He was confident, cool, had an amazing double-handed forehand, and didn't give a crap about me. But like any good codependent-in-the-making, the more he resisted, the more I chased, and when I finally got him to make out with me behind the tennis courts at the high school, I was in my glory. I immediately told Jimmy I was breaking up with him—I mean, I had the guy who was the number-one seed, for God's sake!—and Dave immediately never called me again. In fact, I heard he started dating Ms. S.

And so I started high school minus a boyfriend and minus a best friend, all in one. Jimmy gave me the silent treatment for about half the year, and then, finally, after being paired up for a class project together, we both let it go and became best friends again, minus the boyfriend/girlfriend stuff.

All throughout high school, Jimmy was there. He was the

guy on the tennis team who, when we were told to do our daily run, knew to jog straight to the car with me, where we'd jump in when we were out of the coach's sight, jet off to Friendly's for ice cream, gobble it down, park again, and run back down to the courts as if we'd completed the two-mile run. Nothing brings two people together like a Fribble.

Jimmy even had a way of making the uncool seem cool. When I cracked open my high school yearbook recently, I laughed out loud when I read that Jimmy and I were members of the "Emerson Lake and Palmer Music Appreciation Society." As the only two members of the fictional club, Jimmy and I threw in the face of all the cheerleaders, football players, and other conventional members of the student body that it was okay to be so unhip it hurt. But sometimes our "hip to be square" attitude got us into trouble—not with the administration but with our classmates, and one night it was really clear that it was the two of us against all of them.

Fancying ourselves the music aficionados of the school and experts on all things avant-garde, Jimmy and I somehow convinced the junior class to put us in charge of scouting and hiring a band for our annual ring dance. Sick to death of the typical cover bands hired to play "The Long and Winding Road" and "Color My World" over and over throughout the years, Jimmy and I set out to do something different. We visited every basement and garage in a four-town radius and listened to and assessed every group of longhairs who had ever picked up an instrument. After our exhaustive two-week search—when I sat on dozens of washing machines and endured hundreds of renditions of "Smoke on the Water" while gagging on the stench of stale bong water—we had found the perfect ensemble to play our junior dance. The theme was "Nights in White Satin"—probably picked because the homos in our class thought it was "Knights in White Satin" and it fulfilled one of their kinky Dungeons and Dragons sex fantasies. But, despite the theme, because of Jimmy, me, and our band of choice, *this* would be the dance to remember.

The night of the prom, Jimmy and I arrived fashionably late to the school's festively decorated church-a-gym-a-torium, expecting to see our fellow classmates swaying and boogying to the band we had so carefully chosen. But as we walked into the room, instead of being greeted with bouquets of thanks and tips of the hat, we were greeted with whispers, folded arms, and looks that could have shot daggers. I couldn't feel this much hate if I was hired at this point in my career to do my act at the NAACP Image Awards. Ends up our little band of music makers didn't know any real songs—you know, tunes our classmates had heard on the airwaves of New Haven's WPLR and the more pop-friendly KC101. No, the band we had picked played only long, meandering prog-rock originals that rivaled Jethro Tull's full-album-length *Passion Play* in duration and pomposity. Let's put it this way: They played rock operas that were as about as entertaining as regular operas.

There they were cranking out forty-minute song after forty-minute song about Excalibur or King Arthur or some shit, completely oblivious to the fact that people hated them. I haven't seen a performance that delusional since Howie Mandel hosted the Emmys.

Now, remember: These were the days before girls were contractually obligated to give it up on prom night, so the band was all the attendees had to look forward to. So naturally the entire class blamed us for ruining the prom. And, looking back, they probably had a point. The band was as bad as Winger without the street cred. And while I'd love to say they went on to become REM, I'm pretty sure most of them went on to become drywall hangers with socks stuffed into their leather pants. But at the time, Jimmy and I thought they were the shit. So instead of hanging our heads down and apologizing, what did Jimmy and I do? We held on to our dates, marched right over to our front-and-center table, and sat coolly jamming to the music that no one else was sophisticated and smart enough to appreciate. What plebians! What philistines! *This* was real music! "Their loss," our glances told each other, and even as the Stepford Bitch class president rushed over in a panic to tell us that the band didn't even know how to play the prom theme song by the Moody Blues, Jimmy just shrugged and told her not to sweat it, to just enjoy it. As she stormed off in a huff, her little skinny arms ending in balled-up fists of fury like Mary-Kate Olsen waving away food, I glanced over at Jimmy, whose head was bobbing slowly to the music's meandering beat, his arm slung casually over the back of his date's chair.

"That's how I want to be," I remember thinking. "I want to be like him. I want to make life look that easy."

part three

Comedian,
Heal Thyself!

CHAPTER EIGHT

My Big Fat Italian Bottom—

Tommy and the Crash of 2007

In my life, one thing has always been consistent. Any time I felt like "Wow, all my problems are over," the biggest one was right around the corner. So, on the May day in 2007 when I bought my first four pairs of really expensive shoes—two pairs of Jimmy Choos, two Guccis—I should have known trouble was around the bend. But as I swung the designer bags—logos facing out, of course, so people would know I had money—and headed up to the Comic Strip to perform for a benefit after a sold-out show at the Friars Club, I felt like the world was at my feet. Little did I know,

I would be brought to my knees for the entire following year.

"Can I put those in the office for you?"

Those were the first words Tommy spoke to me, and for the rest of the evening, it seemed like every time I turned around, there he was—at my elbow while I watched the other comics from the back of the room, at the bar where the comics got their drinks, watching my set from the booth. The guy was near me so much that night I got a cramp from holding in my farts. It wasn't until I was halfway home to Connecticut that his comment—"Hey, if you ever decide to dump that Spanish guy, give me a call"—struck me as something he may have said seriously.

I called my friend/stylist, Andy, to check the facts. Could a guy that cute, that *white*, be flirting with me? I knew I'd lost a bunch of the weight I'd put on after my breakup with Darryl, but still, I had to call her to confirm my suspicions.

Andy is a *gorgeous* woman and was one of my only happily married friends. I told her about Tommy's attentiveness, his hailing of my cab, his come-on, and asked her opinion. Ever the love addict and romantic, Andy gushed, "Oh, my God, he likes you. You should call him." So, in a combination of revenge against the emotionally unavailable Latino from Chicago I was seeing and a compulsive need to have this seemingly emotive Italian in my life, I devised a plan to see if he could put his money where his mouth was. Or, as I prefer, my pussy where his mouth was.

❁

"Hey, J.R., it's Lisa Lampanelli," I told the club manager the next day when I called from Houston, where I'd flown less than twelve hours after the show at the Strip. "I was wondering if I could get the name of your Tommy—I may need some security." Knowing full well that I was full of it, J.R., who was, unbeknownst to me at the time, Tommy's best friend, readily gave out the number.

I dialed the 917 exchange and crossed my fingers. When Tommy answered and I told him it was me, he later told me he literally jumped up and down with joy. "Just ask my friend Steve," he said a few days later as we sat talking on the phone for what must have been the fifteenth time in three days. "I couldn't believe it was you—I was so *happy*!" Well, that's all I needed to hear to send me into full-tilt "in love" mode. I had found the love of my life—I just knew it. I didn't care that he was a struggling comic (the number-one entry on my brand-new list of dating no-nos) or that he ended most of our conversations with the statement "I gotta go smoke a blunt with Steve" (entry number three). He was nearly giddy at the thought of me! With that one sentence, the rule book went out the window. And let's face it, my rule book is consulted less than the one for Candyland. When I say "Don't date a struggling comic or drug user," the unspoken end of that sentence is "unless they're reasonably attractive or show any interest in me whatsoever."

And so began the year of Tommy—also known as the Year of Darkness. Now, before you misunderstand and think I'm putting all the blame on Tommy, let me make this clear. There's a saying I heard in a therapy group once that went "Every time I got screwed, I got into position." Sure, Tommy may have stuck it in—metaphorically and physically speaking—but for a year, there I was, ass in the air and begging for it. What

I'm trying to say is it takes two, motherfucker, and he had me at the word "blow." Sadly, I now wish that "blow" was in reference to drugs.

For our first date, we arranged to meet at the New York Hilton bar, where I got a room upstairs—just in case I got tipsy and couldn't drive home to Connecticut or, even better, if we both got a little tipsy and wanted to make out. And make out we did! From the second we met outside the hotel—which felt like a reunion right out of *The Way We Were*, complete with giddiness that can only result from hours and hours of late-night conversations—to hours later, in my favorite martini bar. There, among the velvet furniture and dark green walls, we tipped back a few even though I *never* drink, watched videos on Tommy's portable player—his constant companion—and kissed and kissed and kissed. My head was spinning like rims on an Escalade, and I was in love. His voice mail message to me the next day saying, "New York misses you already," sealed the deal. He was the one—this was the one who would make my life complete and the search would be over.

As any addict does, I chased the high. I will explain. Ask anyone who's ever used heroin or cocaine, and they'll tell you that that first high is the best high of their life, and their continued use of the substance is their effort to recapture that special way they felt when they first used. Well, from the time I took my first hit of Tommy, I was hooked. But like any other drug, the second high didn't quite live up to that first hit, and for the next year, I chased and chased but soared less and less every day.

First, there were the unanswered phone calls at carefully prearranged times. Then there was the fact that Tommy wanted to keep our relationship a secret so no one would think he was dating me to get ahead in the business. A secret? What am I— your girlfriend or a genital wart? By the time he canceled a date with me because it was "pouring out," I was frustrated, furious, and more focused than ever on making this pot-smoking, minimum-wage-earning, emotionally distant thirty-six-year-old mine. He was the prize, damn it, and I was going to win him. Now I understand why rednecks spend fifty bucks at a fair to win a Lynyrd Skynyrd mirror worth a nickel.

Looking back, I don't hate Tommy. He was what he was, and he did the best he could, given his tumultuous upbringing, mixed messages from his parents, and distrust of all things psychological. I feel for him and hope that one day he works on his issues and finds what he needs to be happy. However, at the time, the mood swings he stirred in me from sunup to sundown so mirrored the ups and downs of my childhood in a challenging, turbulent household, he was simply irresistible. Now, after a few years of therapy on the subject, I can see that he was the most lethal combination of my parents' bad traits, minus most of their good qualities. He alternately ignored me, worshipped me, adored me, yelled at me, shamed me, and stormed out on me—not that those are necessarily *bad* things, they just didn't work for me. So naturally, he was my drug, my tonic. Besides, he was hot, charismatic (what pothead isn't?), tons of fun, and had those adorable puppy dog eyes that sucked me in every time. And he was my first hot white guy ever. I was obsessed.

And so began a year that can only be described as hell. Sleepless nights, innumerable ultimatums, pot-induced nausea and headaches, and the internal push and pull that happens only when you do something you know is absolutely wrong for you and, no matter how hard you try, can't find words to defend it. Dating Tommy was like stepping in dog shit and then telling your friends your feet have never felt softer.

My friends begged me to stop seeing him, I snapped and lashed out at innocent people, and I hid it all from my family (the first sign that things ain't good). We broke up, made up, decided to be "just friends," and made out despite being just friends in such a rapid cycle that from one day to the next our status was a mystery even to us. All the while, I tried to push stories I'd heard of Tommy's indiscretions out of my head, and I tried to justify that I was dating other people too and hiding it because of my own sense of self-preservation. But no matter how many times I resolved never to speak with him again, my addict had found his addict, and under no circumstances would either one of us let go.

❁

By the following April, I received a wake-up call. It was the day before the Andy Dick roast on the Howard Stern show, and I had not written draft one of my segment. Now, those of you who have read anything about me know that Howard Stern is the most important person to me professionally—the person whose opinion I value most. Here I was, the night before a big show on Stern, and I hadn't even put pen to paper, due to my obsession with my great unattainable love. Looking back, I still feel a pit in my stomach thinking what I had risked—the respect of the man I value most in the world, plus the disappointment of Stern fans, the fans who were consistently allowing me to sell out venues all over the country.

Fortunately for me, Andy Dick is so fucked up the jokes actually wrote themselves. And thankfully, by the grace of God, I killed at the roast. But I knew I had to get out of this "relationship" before I hurt the only thing I felt I had: my career. Tommy had to go.

I sent Tommy an e-mail. Of course, it was one of my classics, full of pithy phrases plucked from choice episodes of *Sex and the City*—I was sure he didn't watch it and so would not guess the source of the references—and from the bestselling book *He's Just Not That Into You*. In so many words, my Carrie told his Mr. Big that he needed to work on himself for a year, decide what he wanted, and then see if I was still available. The letter was full of melodrama—like the relationship itself—and I wished him well, telling him I could not speak with him for sixty days so that I could heal.

Never one to follow rules, Tommy called and e-mailed, and for a while, I resisted. But on the night of the Washington, D.C., premiere of *Delta Farce*, which I attended with friends and management, he sent the e-mail to end all e-mails, with a song attached: "The Reason" by Hoobastank. Now, for those of you who aren't familiar with "The Reason," it belongs in chapter 1 of *The Addict's Manual to Winning the Bitch Back*. Between the line about being sorry about the pain he caused and the one about me being the reason he changed, the song was my manipulator's secret weapon.

As I downloaded and listened to the tune in my condo in Connecticut, my mind raced. "Oh, my God! He's admitting it—he's admitting he's not a perfect person and that he did bad things to me. But he wants to start over new—and the reason is *me*!!" I couldn't have felt more like a rescuer if I worked for the ASPCA. Not only that, but "Hoobastank" was his nickname for my coochie, so there was some sentimentality involved. Score one point for Tommy—mission accomplished!

A day later, I picked up the phone, and so did he. (Funny how most of the times we were broken up, he heard the phone, but when we were dating, he couldn't seem to hear it. But that's neither here nor there.) I agreed, after several heart-wrenching conversations, to get back together with him if he A) would go into couple's therapy with me; and B) told the world, including all his MySpace friends (it really *did* seem important at the time), that we were a couple. I would not be someone's dirty little secret, and we needed to come out of the closet. Tommy agreed.

Little did Tommy know, I planned to "out" us as a couple in a big way. Having scheduled an appearance on the Stern show for a week later, I asked Tommy to accompany me to the Sirius studios. Of course, he agreed. A huge Stern fan and a major opportunist, as is every comedian I've ever met including myself, he couldn't wait and was at the hotel early to come over to the studios with me.

As I sat on the couch dishing with Stern—who loves when I talk about dating the blacks—I dropped a bombshell: I, Lisa Lampanelli, the girl who's "blown more black guys than Hurricane Katrina," was dating a white guy. Howard couldn't believe it. It was true, I insisted. He's here—in the greenroom— I told the King of All Media. Well, that's all it took for Howard to call Tommy into the studio and up to the microphone. Our relationship was no longer a secret; we were out in the open—the headliner and the pothead, the rich girl and the guy with no checking account. If you had animated us as cats, we could have been a classic Disney film.

Was I happy? You'd think so, huh?

I had the guy I'd been pushing to be in a relationship with for over a year, and I had his full disclosure on the biggest national radio show in the world. The problem was: Now that I had him, did I really want him, and why?

Here's an analogy for you: Tommy was like a Krispy Kreme doughnut. You dream about eating one, drive yourself crazy with the anticipation, and then you buy a dozen. The first one is sweet but goes down way too fast and the memory of how great it was quickly fades. By doughnut four, you're a little disgusted with yourself. How could you have made such a big deal about something that ain't really that cool? By the end of the box, you're just sick to your stomach and want to puke. That's how I felt about Tommy.

It's really just as simple as that. I mean, here I was, a millionaire with five thousand dollars' worth of fake hair, a chinchilla coat, and a large collection of funny dresses. Plus I wasn't even enormously fat anymore, having lost about thirty pounds on Jenny Craig, and I was dating a wigger hundredaire whose farts reeked so much of pot smoke they made me crave brownies.

Seriously, though, a funny thing had started happening—my self-esteem had started growing a bit in those past few months, and I'd started wondering: Is this the best I can do?

Can't I do better than dating the less successful half of Cheech and Chong? How the fuck do I get better looking and more successful and date worse guys? Hell, at this rate, if I get my own sitcom, I'll probably marry Beetlejuice!

I mean, I'm fucking the guy who answers the phone at the Comic Strip! What's the matter—the guy who cleans the toilets at Dangerfield's was taken?!? The phone answerer at the Strip? That's one step below the guy who mops up at a peep show. It's pretty fucking sad when the best thing you can say about your boyfriend is that he's great at conference calling. Seriously, Muslim prostitutes are more respected in their communities. I'm a star and this guy's on the lowest rung of the show business ladder. It's clear—I'm officially dating the Italian K-Fed.

Only hours after the morning broadcast, I started to have doubts. Seriously, *a few hours*! People ask me when I knew it was over with Tommy, and I always say, "That afternoon." No shit. Back at Tommy's seedy second-floor railroad apartment in Queens, we listened to the replay of the show. Tommy was laughing it up, and I was trying to push our latest fight out of my head. Right after the taping, we'd gotten into an argument because he wanted us to stay at his apartment in Queens— which, by the way, had had some plumbing problems so that the shower and bathroom were completely overflowing with sewage—and I wanted to have us stay at the hotel, a four-star place Lionsgate Pictures put me up in for the movie I was promoting. Tommy had gotten hugely pissed that I didn't want to stay at Chez Shit—with the plumbing problems, no air-conditioning, and cat hair (what kind of a guy has a cat anyway?)—and I wanted us to stay in a junior suite on Park Avenue. Either pot was on the way or somehow the smell of urine helped him sleep better. The apartment was such a mess that when you took a dump, it was considered a renovation. But I tried to understand his point: I mean, who wants to stay in a luxury hotel when you could stay in a three-room apartment with the only bathroom in the world where you're dirtier when you get *out* of the shower? It would've been more sanitary to take a bath in his toilet.

As we listened to the replay, I heard Howard ask me why a woman like me would chase a guy like him: a pothead with no checking account, no driver's license, no self-esteem, and anger issues—pretty much Gary Busey without the moments of clarity, the talent, and the money. In short, Tommy had more problems than an algebra textbook and the answers weren't listed in the back.

So Howard asked me why I would be with a guy like him, and I said without missing a beat, "Profound self-hate." Of course, Howard, Artie, and the whole crew laughed, but when I listened to the replay that afternoon, it dawned on me that that sentence was the most real thing I'd said the whole show. At that moment, I knew I had to break it off. I mean, when your boyfriend's the biggest addict in a room with Artie Lange, you've got a real problem on your hands.

At that moment, my mind started to go back through our whole relationship, even that short part of it after I agreed to take him back just a week prior. During our first counseling session, he'd stormed out of the shrink's office, a sure sign that the "anything" he'd agreed to do to get me back had its limits. Then I remembered that when I was flying in for our big reunion, he asked what airport I was flying into, and I said Newark. He said, "Wow, it's a shame you're not flying into LaGuardia. Newark's too far to come meet you. But don't worry, I'll be sitting here waiting for you when you come back." Wow! Lemme get this straight. You'll be *sitting* and *waiting* for me? Thank you, Mr. Wonderful! Pardon me while I swoon. What was his motto? "Love means never having to take the PATH train"? If I flew into his living room, he'd probably complain it was too far from the bedroom. I guess the "anything" he'd do for me meant he'd follow me to the ends of the earth, as long as there wasn't a bridge or tunnel on the way. I couldn't help but remember a few years back when my Internet fix-up, Darryl, had picked me up at Newark Airport with a huge bouquet of flowers, and we hadn't even met yet! But I digress: In Tommy's defense, I must point out that there *was* an *America's Funniest Home Videos* marathon on TV that night. *AFHV* is to a stoner what *Gone with the Wind* is to your grandmother.

The day after the Stern show, things got worse. I did the self-hate "joke" again on Adam Carolla's radio show and when Tommy overheard it, it really hurt his feelings. So now, not only was I hurting myself, I was hurting him. Then we got into a raging fight that night because I wanted to go to the movies sober and he wanted to smoke beforehand. Of course, the movie in question was *Delta Farce,* so I probably should have listened to him. How could I continue to date a guy I wanted to change this much? This shit wasn't meant to be.

Two days later, Tommy laughingly told me he heard Gary,

Howard's producer, on the *Wrap-Up Show* saying he couldn't wait until we broke up in a year so that they could play the clips of us acting all lovey-dovey and make fun of us. I thought to myself, "A year! You better take the under." Then it dawned on me that I hadn't had the guts to tell any of my friends or family that we were back together. I had only told my equally codependent friend Tracy, who kept saying how great we were together because she's a hopeless romantic—I mean, the bitch *still* holds out hope for Liza Minnelli and David Gest—and is afraid to be alone too. My friend Laura—who later told me she was "this close" to staging a Tommy intervention—said she'd heard us on the show together and that we sounded happy. I burst into tears and said I was anything but happy, and I couldn't think of anything I liked about him other than the fact that he was cute and was good in the sack. Hell, I could have had just as much fun with a kitten and a vibrator. I didn't trust him because of his bullshit commitment issues over the past year, and I couldn't let it go. I mean, this guy drove me so nuts that I'm surprised I didn't join NASA and drive cross-country wearing an adult diaper. And don't get me wrong: It wasn't like I was looking for marriage. I knew Tommy wouldn't get down on one knee unless his hash pipe rolled under the kitchen table. But still, by the time we got back together, I didn't believe he was committed and had an enormous list of stuff for him to change about himself. This wasn't fair to him or to me.

Add to this the fact that he brought out the absolute worst in me. Before I dated Tommy, I never had a boyfriend who said I was jealous, clingy, or insecure. But our lethal combination was just the ticket to make me all three. Tommy had a string of ten or fifteen women he kept around as "friends" but were women he had slept with, wanted to sleep with, or who he'd do in a pinch, who called at all hours of the night and texted constantly, and he would not tell them to leave him alone. This guy got more creepy e-mails than Chris Hansen. It's like he was developing a whole minor league of whores that he could call up at any time and I was the aging slugger.

Now, knowing psychology a little, I know this is just because he had an abandonment complex and could never be alone. But it showed his lack of commitment and concentration on *our* relationship and brought out a jealous side that I had never had, and I admit, I acted *ridiculously*! I even checked his e-mail once when he was sleeping and found out about all these women—a fact that I admitted to in therapy and he never let me hear the end of. Of course, it was exactly like the guy whose wife hires a private eye and finds out he's having an affair, and the husband focuses on the fact that she hired the private eye instead of taking responsibility for the affair. It was like being blamed for ruining an anal rape by farting.

I joke about it, but I hated my behavior. And I couldn't remember once in thirty-three years of dating having ever been jealous. So I called a few of my ex-boyfriends and asked them if they remembered me being jealous, insecure, or downright crazy. And guess what they said? They said I was in violation of the restraining order. No, I kid. They said I was never like that. Even Darryl, my black ex-boyfriend who cheated on me for two months before our breakup, said I was never once insecure or jealous. In fact, I'm sure that's why he found it so easy to cheat—because I trusted him, didn't question him, and had never done so much as look in his wallet. The only way I caught him was when our phone bill came and there were $600 worth of phone calls to the same number in one month at all hours. I knew his parole officer didn't work nights, and I knew it wasn't the customer service line for Afro Sheen, so it was obviously another woman.

So, after talking to these exes, I realized that Tommy and I brought out the worst in each other—his flirting and just-short-of-cheating behavior made me act insane and jealous, and my insanity and jealousy made him more distant, creating a vicious cycle.

I had an emergency session with my shrink. He told me something I will always remember—and I quote: "If my daughter came home with a guy like him, I would be suicidal." And believe me, I know. I was two seconds from pulling an Owen Wilson myself. But I was addicted to him, and I couldn't cut him off. And his compelling codependent arguments for us maintaining contact—like "You said you'd never delete me," "You said we were family," and my personal favorite, "You're a cunt and nobody will ever love you like I do"—made it impossible for me to quit him.

Not that I didn't try. I escaped for a week and went to Canyon Ranch. When I got back to my room after faking my way through yet another Chi Gong class, there was a string of messages from Tommy:

BEEP: "You know, you're a real cunt. I can't believe you won't return my calls. You said you'd always love me and once again, you won't even pick up. Fine—I hate you and never want to talk to you again." BEEP: "You know, I know you have another boyfriend. You must—or this wouldn't be so easy for you. Here I am, sitting here alone, waiting for you to call me back, and you're off at your fuckin' cult place, taking your 'Forget Tommy' classes. Well, fuck you. I hope you die." BEEP: "I'm just not myself. [*sniff*] I'm sorry. I could never hate you. [*sniff*] Please call me back. I'm waiting here. I love you. Call me . . . please . . . I love you . . . you're not a cunt."

Now, I don't know about you gals out there, but for me, there's nothing more romantic than a guy saying you're not a cunt. In fact, I think he stole that from a Cameron Crowe film. It's a Hallmark moment. "Oooh, that's hot, honey. Now tell me I'm not a loudmouthed twat."

It was such a love/hate codependent thing. One night, I was on my way to a show and got two messages from friends saying, "Who's Tommy and why has he requested me as a friend on MySpace?" He was actually trolling my MySpace page for friends—and, of course, by *coincidence*, he was only contacting the good-looking girls. I'm in the limo *furious*, raging about it to my buddy, when I get a text from Tommy saying, "I love you." And, without missing a beat and still in midscream, I text back, "I love you too, honey." Send. When it came to Tommy, all logic went out the window, like with crack. But really, this guy was worse than crack. Crack disappears after you smoke it—it doesn't go on your MySpace page and troll for hot chicks.

That was it! I could never talk to this guy again! But how? I realized for the first time in my adult life that I needed help, I needed answers, and I didn't have either.

I had hit my bottom, and I had no idea how to claw my way out.

CHAPTER NINE

Comedy's Lovable Queen of Denial

ince I started doing comedy around 1990, I have taken very few vacations. I am a workaholic who finally found her passion, so what need did I have for time away? I loved what I did, I did what I loved, and that was enough for me. Only in the past few years, I had found that it wasn't enough. The work was taking care of itself, with more fame and fortune coming my way on what seemed like a monthly basis, but I was finding myself growing dissatisfied with my dead-end relationships and my weight fluctuation. But until I bottomed out in 2007 in the most toxic relationship of my adult life, I let it all slide. I was on autopilot—work, eat, date, work, diet, date—until it all came to a crashing halt and I was forced to take the vacation nobody wants to take. No, not the in-laws' house, Darfur, or gay pride weekend at Disney World. I was going to spend my vacation in rehab.

For more than a year, I had driven myself insane with my relationship with Tommy, and I had no idea how to get out. I had found out in therapy that I was a caregiver, a rescuer, and every time Tommy said he couldn't live without me, I simply couldn't let go. Just so you understand, caregivers are people who have such low self-esteem that they grab on to people beneath them—in my case, addicts, ex-cons, middle acts—and try to make them better people to prove their own self-worth. Of course, now I know better. I know if I feel the need to rescue something, I should adopt a dog or volunteer for the Special Olympics. This makes sense. Unfortunately, back in June of 2007, when I was still enmeshed with Tommy, I was more unstable than that bridge in Minnesota, and I didn't know how to break the vicious cycle.

Oprah is always talking about angels, and even though I'd begun to drift away from her in the past few years, I agreed with something she said. My angel came to me one night in L.A. in the form of a skinny singer/songwriter with jet-black dyed hair and nine years of sobriety. My angel was Joie.

I was in L.A. about to do *The Tonight Show* for the fourth time, and I should have been on top of the world. Jay Leno liked me—something I never thought would happen in this lifetime, due to my edgy, blue material—and my weight was finally under control. Unfortunately, I could not say the same for my codependent relationship with Tommy.

Sitting having dinner at the Hollywood Improv, I felt special. Since I hadn't been to the Melrose club in several years, I was given the celebrity treatment—a corner table in the dining room, an incredibly attentive waiter, free dessert, and an offer to do a spot, which I turned down since it was my night off. But inside, I still felt ill at ease. I was wrestling with the idea of maintaining contact with Tommy, even though the toxicity of the relationship rivaled that of a New Jersey landfill—or a New Jersey playground, for that matter.

Of course, when you're obsessed with someone, that's all you can think and talk about, and even though I had just met Joie (pronounced Joey) that night, I was already spilling my guts to him about this horror show of a relationship.

". . . so I really think we can be friends. I mean, I know he sent pictures of his dick to other women, but we weren't even going out at the time. He was just trying to get me to go back out when that happened, so it's okay that he sent the pictures, right? And I think even though we can't date, we can still be friends," I said to the man with the kind eyes I'd just met.

Writing this now, I know how ridiculous it sounds. I want to puke just thinking about it.

But Joie didn't puke—he didn't even judge.

All he said was, "Uh-oh, you've got it bad."

Then, instead of going off on me and telling me how stupid I was, he told me in a very even tone and calm voice a story of his own, about a girl he had been in a similar Tommy-like position with, a girl he knew he could never speak to again. I'd been told stories like this before, most recently by my poor beleaguered friend Laura, who tried hard day after day not to preach to me or scold me. But something about Joie's empathy and compassion rolled up in a story so similar to my own made me think. And it helped me make a decision.

Joie was right—I could never talk to Tommy again.

But how? I asked. Sure, I could start by changing his name in my cell phone to "Prick" so that every time he called, I would remember two things—what a prick he was and the fact that he sent pictures of his prick to other women. And I could block him from my e-mail and MySpace pages. But these were all too easy—temporary fixes. I had to figure out why I was attracted to Tommy in the first place and never, ever let it happen again.

And so began my first of three stints in rehab.

Now, when people think of rehab, they think of one of two things: drugs or alcohol. Unfortunately, what I was going to rehab for was neither hip nor cool, nor did it have the edgy, dark qualities of heroin or liquor. The first rehab I checked into was to treat me for codependency. In fact, the minute Joie told me about the famous Caron Foundation's codependency program, I knew I would go. Rushing home from the Improv, I fired up my computer and left the intake counselor three urgent messages, and when she called me back, I plunked down three thousand bucks on the spot. It wasn't until I hung up the phone that I realized I was scared shitless.

Of course, like everyone else in the world, I thought rehab would look like a cross between *One Flew over the Cuckoo's Nest* and *Girl, Interrupted,* minus the star power of patients like Jack and Angelina, and without the sexual tension and Academy Awards. I imagined enormous white metal doors that would shut behind me with a loud thud, followed by the sharp click of a lock, behind which I would be trapped and eventually either tortured, electroshocked, or both. I summoned up images of patients in white hospital gowns rocking back and forth in an effort to soothe themselves, and images of me, frightened, sitting in a corner, crying silently, begging to go home.

As I drove to the place where I was to spend the next five days, these snapshots swam through my head. But as I headed into the town of Wernersville, Pennsylvania, I had a pleasant surprise. Instead of a razor-wired asylum, there stood a charming, if not perfectly kept up, old farmhouse, surrounded by a huge front porch, complete with rocking chairs and a smoking pit in the back. Still, as I parked my car, my heart was racing, and even though I knew I was doing what was best for me, this would be anything but easy.

"You promise to pick up if I call?" I begged my friend Laura for reassurance over the phone as I lingered in the car, stealing a few more minutes of freedom before I entered the farmhouse's back door. Promising me once more that she most certainly would—as she had the dozen or so times I had asked her the same question during the anxiety-ridden week before—I felt her warmth across the miles. "This place is going to be good for you or Joie wouldn't have told you about it," she reminded me. Laura, no stranger to psychiatric hospitals in her youth, told me it would in no way be like a bad movie about mental illness, and looking around in the driveway, I knew she was right.

It turns out there was really nothing creepy about rehab. The only remotely uncomfortable thing was that roommates were mandatory. I hadn't shared a room with anyone except a boyfriend since my college days, and I wasn't thrilled about going back to it now. My roommate was Shelley, an eating-disordered codependent who kept piles of affirmation books on her bedside table. I knew immediately she wasn't one of the "cool kids" there, and I set out to find the A list, the people I could bond with, smoke with (I didn't smoke cigarettes, but the occasional Black and Mild would make me feel like I fit in), and form lifelong post-rehab friendships with.

Within a few hours, I met Heather, Jill, John, and Brett, who eventually put two and two together and figured out who I was. As with all rehabs, the place is anonymous—hence our referring to ourselves by first names only. But I made sure to slip in a coupla Chink jokes and enough details about my life and use my onstage voice when speaking so that it started to dawn on them that I was Comedy's Lovable Queen of Mean. Thank God! That way, I could feel a little more special than the rest of the group. I mean, I may be codependent, but I'd be damned if I wasn't gonna be the most famous codependent at Caron that week and receive all the perks being the celebrity brings—like extra Jell-O.

And bond we did. Despite being cautioned not to hang out exclusively with one group and threatened with dismissal if any physical or sexual boundaries were crossed, the five of us broke those rules. But how could we help it? I mean, I was semifamous, Jill and Heather were smokin' hot, Brett was employed as a sommelier in one of New York City's finest restaurants, and John was a good-looking baby-faced sweet-heart with several years of sobriety under his belt. We were, in short, Caron's version of *St. Elmo's Fire* without that chubby dud Mare Winningham.

The five of us did everything together. We ate together,

we played games together, and after ten-hour days of therapy, we stayed up until all hours of the night, discussing our own codependency and our failed relationships and calling each other on our shit. Sure, the group therapy, the lectures, and the psychodramas (physically and emotionally draining role-playing sessions where we acted out and purged our childhood traumas) were helpful. But the connection of our little group seemed to do much more. By day three, I felt like I'd known these people for years. I knew more about them than I did my family. I knew I was in the right place.

The only person outside our little group who intrigued me was Peter. Peter was an older guy—probably around fifty or so—who had rugged good looks; a tan that I imagined came from boating on Long Island, where he lived; and eyes that said he was really listening to you. Many years sober, Peter, with his steamy, quiet ways, was irresistible to me, and I just had to know what his story was.

Now, in rehab, the members of group therapy are forbidden from disclosing what happens in their individual group to members of other groups, to discourage loss of confidentiality. But Jill was in Peter's group, and I set about finding out if he could be the next Mr. Lampanelli. Unfortunately, what I found out wasn't good. Not only was Peter married, Peter had forty-seven wives—that is, he was married to a woman with forty-seven different personalities, and he had come to Caron to get up the strength to leave her. Now, let that sink in, bitches! Forty-seven personalities! His wife had more flavors than Baskin-Robbins. Of course, at the time they got married, Peter's wife had had only one personality—I assume a pretty good one or he wouldn't have married her—but she had suffered a trauma in which her personality split into almost four dozen people, some of them children and babies! In fact, her multiple personalities were so involved and confusing that Peter carried a chart around with him just so he could keep track, a chart I refer to as the Periodic Table of the Elements of Crazy.

Now, a few months earlier, Peter would have seemed perfect for me. He was an ideal candidate for me to rescue! But, as they say in twelve-step programs, you can't unlearn what you know, and after all I'd learned about my codependence and after bottoming out with Tommy, I ran for my life. Besides, I wasn't about to piss off a woman with forty-seven personalities—that's a hell of a lot of heckling if she ever decided to come out to one of my shows! She would have been harder to kill than the Terminator.

Speaking of Tommy, by the time I'd arrived at rehab in late June, it had been a week since I'd returned any of his calls or texts. I had blocked him from my e-mail as I knew I should, but I'd be damned if I was gonna change my phone number and give him that power. So, like clockwork, three days into my stay, just as I was beginning to get something out of the program, there were two of his trademark manipulative messages on my voice mail. Even though the therapists were on lunch break, I frantically stormed into my shrink Rick's office and asked to speak with him.

"Well, if you're going to return those calls, you might as well leave right now," Rick said, hard-lining me. I wasn't going to return them, I assured Rick. I was never speaking to him again! "Well, I seriously advise you to hand in your phone so any more messages or texts don't disturb your progress here."

Hand in my phone? But don't you know who I am, Rick? I'm Lisa Lampanelli, Comedy's Lovable Queen of Mean! I'm almost famous! I have a career, goddamn it! Rick shrugged, unfazed. "Well, if you listen to any more messages he leaves, you're just dialing for pain."

I'm happy to say I didn't dial for pain at Caron, and I haven't done so for more than sixteen months as I sit here writing this book. In fact, after leaving Caron, I was advised not to date for a year since my addiction to men was what had gotten me in there to begin with. So, even though I'd gone dateless for a year before I decided to sample the chocolate love a few years back, I knew I needed to give it a rest once again. I agreed with the powers that be at Caron; I definitely wouldn't date. I would take an entire twelve-month period to work on myself, I'd buy a crate of batteries at Costco for my vibrator, and I'd do something about my "picker"—as in "When it comes to picking men, my picker is out of whack." I knew that year would give me a lot of time to do stuff I'd wanted to do for a while. I mean, with my mind on men all the time, I hadn't had time to revisit the piano—one of my favorite pastimes in my teens. I hadn't had the energy to join a tennis league or get a singing coach. In fact, now that I wasn't dating, maybe I'd have time to write my highly anticipated Broadway show *Best Little Whorehouse in Connecticut,* or, even better, *Code-pendency: The Musical,* with the big closing number "Boy, Is My Cunt Tired." I mean, I'd hardly had any breaks from dating since I was twelve—that's almost thirty-four years of holding in farts while trying to pretend I'm a "lady." And when it comes to sex, what can I tell you? My vag had been more backed up than midtown at rush hour. And where, oh where, had all this dating gotten me? The guy got good sex, but what did I get? A yeast infection and a pinched nerve in my neck. No more dating for me! Time to wash those men right outta my snatch!

Sounds like a good plan, huh? Sure it does—*on paper*! See, what I didn't count on was loneliness. I didn't see it coming and it hit me like a ton of bricks. This was especially true on Friday and Saturday nights—"date night" for the rest of the population. It was on those nights, when I saw couples in the audience, that I was most tempted to rustle up some male companionship.

And then something occurred to me: Just because I'm not allowed to date doesn't mean I'm not allowed to fuck. Caron never said anything about just fucking. Why didn't I think of this before?

So, during the summer after Caron, I spent my days at Canyon Ranch health spa, crying when I needed to, reading self-help books, eating healthy food, and when the loneliness became too painful to face, I read my fan mail and lined up some dates—er, I mean, fucks.

Around August, I couldn't take the aloneness anymore. I'd had enough. Enough attempts at yoga class and meditation at Canyon Ranch. Enough of sporadically attended twelve-step meetings. And enough of staring at hot guys, unable to take any action whatsoever. So instead of picking up my recently ordered copy of *Healing Your Aloneness* and *The Healing Your Aloneness Workbook,* I printed out an e-mail from a hot little Mexican/Italian mix—not terribly unlike Tommy in appearance, now that I think about it—who coincidentally enough lived in Vegas, where I was going to tape *Larry the Cable Guy's*

Christmas Spectacular. You know what they say: "What happens in Vegas . . ." Wow! This was great. Not only did I get to fly to Vegas to bang hot little guinea/spic Johnny, VH1 was financing the whole thing. I mean, what could possibly go wrong in Vegas for a person fighting addictions?

In case you ever need it, here is the exact recipe for loneliness:

1. Spend two sexless, dateless months at a health spa frequented by women who at every turn are happier, skinnier, prettier, more satisfied, and in general, just plain better than you;

2. Add one first-class flight and a gorgeous suite at the Palms Resort Casino in Las Vegas;

3. Pepper with the artificial ego rush of being in Sin City to shoot a nationally aired TV special for a good friend;

4. Garnish with being surrounded by showgirls, high rollers, and other Vegas accoutrements that send all recently learned recovery skills out the window.

That, my friends, can add up to nothing but loneliness, and that's where Johnny came in.

Johnny actually wasn't anything like Tommy. He was half-Mexican and half-white—which I guess means he still gets harassed at the border, but eventually gets let in—and he and I had dinner and he *paid.* Having not had a guy pay for dinner since the time Tommy asked me to cash his paycheck so it could be his treat at the diner, I was excited. So excited that I gave Johnny a little outside-the-pants action—hey, you gotta check under the hood before you take it for a test drive—and he went home. Since the dress rehearsal had gone well, I couldn't wait for opening night.

Unlike Tommy too, he called the next day and asked what I was doing. Even though I was exhausted, my need for human contact outweighed my need for sleep. I told him I had a break from taping around two that afternoon, so he agreed to drive me to Caesars' Forum Shops so I could go to Jimmy Choo. Little did I know, Johnny thought Jimmy Choo was a Chinese restaurant and appeared disappointed when I told him he was to accompany me while I went shoe shopping. He was looking forward to the #11 Hunan Beef, and I was looking for a pair of size 10s.

After a full morning of rehearsals for the special, I hurried up to my room and made sure I was fresh as a daisy—well, at least as fresh as a daisy that wants to get laid. I was in the mood to shop a bit and impress Johnny with how I bought $500 pairs of shoes without looking at the price tag. I know—most women put out so men will buy them expensive gifts. I get turned on if there's a straight guy in the room when I buy my own. Then, I planned, I would bring him up to my hotel for a little up-close-and-personal inside-the-pants action. I mean, it was our second meeting. It was time.

Ends up I wasn't the only one who had an agenda in mind. As I climbed into Johnny's SUV, he suggested a quick detour to pick up someone else. At first I thought, "Man, this spic is so lazy he's picking up a day worker to do his foreplay!" Hold on, though! A threesome? I've never had one of those. But no, Johnny's plan didn't include a threesome or sex of any kind.

"Do you mind if we pick up my son at camp?" The bomb-shell dropped. "He's off for the summer and has nowhere to go, so do you mind if he comes with us?" My first thought was "Red flag! He's a Mexican with only one kid. He's gay." But as he looked at me with his pleading little puppy dog eyes and kissed me on the lips, I agreed. Of course, my daydreams of afternoon delight faded, and in their place, there was Ma-dame Tussauds Wax Museum and FAO Schwarz, accompa-nied by Johnny and his eight-year-old offspring. At this point, it would be safe to say that the only thing stiff I touched that day was Elvis's finger.

I was pissed. I was in Vegas, I was lonely, and I was really in the mood to make out. That cockblocker of a kid really cramped my style. So I let Johnny's next three calls go to voice mail. Then I got a message that was worth returning.

Johnny said he had heard I was going to be playing in San Jose the same weekend he was going there to see his father. Of course, I found this fascinating—I mean, he was Hispanic and I couldn't believe he knew who his father was. In any case, we made plans to go to a party I was hosting at a club that Friday, and then to my show on Saturday. For the week before we were to hook up, the texts kept gushing in fast and furious saying how much he was looking forward to seeing me. I was primed!

Anticipating a fun, steamy, and child-free weekend, I landed in San Jose with enough time to shower, change, and look good for the party—and for Johnny. I texted him when I landed, as he had asked me to, and an hour later, I got a text back saying he'd had "a really rough day with his family" and couldn't make it. A rough day with his family! What's a rough day with a spic's family? Too much lettuce to pick? Too tired from selling oranges at the side of the highway? Exhausted from squeezing thirty people into his Chevy to visit the relatives in jail? What happened—the bucket spilled while he was mopping the floor? The lawnmower wouldn't start? He wrecked someone's car while valeting it? (I could go on and on.) Either way, I was pissed—and I headed out of the hotel, ready to replace Johnny with a hotter, steamier, spicier Latino *muy ahora*!

It turns out that Jesus—Jesus our Lord and Savior, not the Hispanic who stole my wallet—was smiling down on me that night. Stepping out of the car at the party, I was introduced to my security guard Fabio, who had to be the hottest Portuguese man I had ever seen.

Now, for those of you who don't know, female comics and security guards go together like chocolate and peanut butter. It's a natural fit. Security guards are always buff, they make you feel protected, and you know where they work in case they steal anything out of your room when you're asleep. Also, they always have handcuffs if you want to get kinky, and they carry a nightstick in case their dicks aren't big enough. Plus, they know where the cameras are hidden so your bare ass doesn't pop up on the Internet.

Well, I personally hadn't banged a security guard in a while, so I figured tonight was the night, thanks to Johnny No-Show.

The times I had hooked up with security guards, it had been fun. It had happened in Houston with Hub, a guy right out of a field-hand fantasy. And it had occurred in West Palm Beach with Pierre, a black guy who was so dumb he must have had a plate in his head—sadly, he was so stupid the plate was Styrofoam. I don't joke when I say this man was so stupid he thought the Jefferson Memorial had statues of George and Weezie in it. But Pierre had served a purpose: he was my rebound bang after my breakup with my black boyfriend Darryl, who had cheated on me, and I'll admit I did it just to prove I still had game. My last security guard encounter had been with a steroid case in Ontario, California, called Thurl, a moniker that I have since learned means "Mama had eighteen kids and ran outta names." Thurl may have had a stupid name, but I basically did him just to see what it would be like to bang a guy *that* buff. Seriously, I chalked that one up to research—sort of like I was Jane Goodall and he was my gorilla in the mist. And just so you don't write me a letter, I know Jane Goodall dealt with chimps and the furthest she ever went with one was a dry hump.

So when I was presented with Fabio the Fabulous that night in San Jose, I knew it was on. It was the old "When one door closes, another one opens," or in this case "When one door closes, you can be pretty sure a spic will jimmy a lock and climb through the window." By the way, I know what you're thinking—a Hispanic security guard? Yeah, I know that's ironic in itself. Putting a spic in charge of security is risky. That's like giving a black guy keys to Popeyes chicken. It's like putting a Chink in charge of driving the bus. But Fabio was what was there, and I was ready to play.

After about three hours of autograph signing, picture taking, and pretending to have fun with some fans, I told Fabio I wanted to leave. He asked what I was doing later, and I took the opening and invited him to my room at the Fairmont.

Rushing back to the hotel, I got ready, giving the underarms and other sensitive areas the ol' Puerto Rican shower. (I wasn't gonna take a full shower for this guy. He was a security guard, for God's sake! I wasn't about to redo my hair and makeup for someone who checks IDs and gives women unnecessary friskings for a living. Plus, I knew my mother would be extra excited if I brought her home some soap from the famous Fairmont hotel.) Plain and simple, I knew this guy was gonna be a one-night stand at the most. Besides, there was really no point in me dating a Portuguese—no one knows stereotypes for the Portuguese, so I wouldn't get any jokes out of the experience. You know what they say: "Once you go Portuguese, you realize it's really hard to find anything that rhymes with 'Portuguese.'" Of course, I tried "Once you go Portuguese, your twat burns when you sneeze," but it never got the laugh I had hoped for.

Twenty minutes later, I answered the door in my robe—a new Lane Bryant bra and black Victoria's Secret XL underwear underneath—and we sat down on the couch together. But instead of making a move, what did Fabio do? He started telling me about himself! What?!? Now, c'mon—it was pretty clear what we were there to do, and I didn't want to hear his life story. I didn't care that his father was a farmer and I sure as hell didn't care that he was the first one in his *familia* to go to college—especially when all he got out of his degree was a job as a security guard. So, after ten minutes of listening to this broken-English fuck, I was like "Tick-toc, spic—we gonna do this or what? Let's get started, 'cause I don't care what your major was. And I don't care how, as a kid, you ate cats and were a water boy for the cockfights."

Now, I'll be honest with you, my dear readers, about one thing. I talk a lot about sex onstage, but I haven't had that much of it—and the sex I have had hasn't been very good. I've been a serial monogamist most of my life, and my brief "ho period" when I discovered black guys was just that—brief. So I haven't been exposed to many weird bedroom customs. Therefore, when Fabio—who was definite eye candy, with tattoos and muscles to his credit (I love that "fresh out of Sing Sing" look)—crouched down next to the side of the bed, I didn't know what to expect.

But instead of doing something I'd seen before—in person or the movies—he shocked the hell out of me. Eyes narrowed, he peered into my nether regions, and he . . . well . . . he . . . spit. Seriously, he spit! What was he trying to do—shine it?!? Now, let me be clear: He didn't wet his fingers and go in for the kill. Nor did he do a little licky thing. He basically was spitting like my snatch was a baseball dugout! All that was missing was that crazy ding noise you hear after someone in a Western hocks one into a nearby brass spittoon. I mean, the guy was spitting on it like my pussy had just insulted his mother!

The first time he did it, I was like, "What the fuck was that?" I'm thinking, "This is really weird." Now, I know guys in prison spit on their stuff, but guys with me don't find that necessary. I may be forty-six, but I have a thirty-year-old's snatch—I'm moist as Betty Crocker down there! It's like riding the log flume. But he kept spitting, and then asked for a review: "You like when I spit on it, don't you?" Of course, I didn't know what to say. I would have loved to be honest, but I didn't want to hurt the feelings of a minimum-wage-earning

Latino who I was never gonna see again. So, I was like, "Uh, yeah," and then I crossed my fingers and rolled my eyes when he wasn't looking, just so I was being true to myself. My integrity is really important to me.

By that point, the evening was ruined for me. I couldn't enjoy myself—the whole time I was completely preoccupied. I kept waiting for him to take out a squeegee, clean it, and ask for a quarter. It was like a carnival game. I figured if he got three in, I'd have to give him a stuffed animal.

After we were done, he tried talking, but I begged off, saying he had to leave because I had to get rest before the big show tomorrow. As I lay there in bed, I started to grasp the truth of the situation: The guys I was attracting *after* codependency rehab—Johnny Vegas, Phlegmy Fabio—were no better than Tommy, my pre-rehab bottom. Despite all the work I'd done on myself, I was still pulling guys who did absolutely nothing for me—physically, psychologically, mentally—and whom I was anything but honest with. At the Caron Foundation, we were taught to ask for our wants and needs, and the last thing I wanted was a guy who brought his kid on a date or one who spit all over my junk.

At that moment, I knew: I had to get back to my year off from men or I'd never get anything better.

Sadly, there was one other thing I noticed when I was heading out on my date with Johnny Vegas and for my night out when I ultimately met Fabio—something that shook me to the core. My pants were too tight. My new "I just lost thirty pounds on Jenny Craig" pants from Ann Taylor Loft were straining at the zipper. At first, I tried to chalk it up to a dry cleaning mishap and succeeded in pushing it out of my mind.

Then as I lay in bed after Fabio's hasty retreat, there was no denying it—the weight I had lost over a year before was coming back. I tried to justify it by saying it was worth a fifteen-pound gain to get rid of Tommy, a 170-pound pain. But there was no excuse for my behavior—sure, I wasn't dating a toxic douchebag, but I was once again using food for comfort as I had all my life. I had replaced one addiction with another.

And, as I lay in bed in San Jose, I realized that I had absolutely no idea what to do about it.

CHAPTER TEN

Fat Girl, Interrupted

"You're not having dessert?" I asked my two friends in disbelief.

"No."

"You've got to be fucking kidding me! You said we were going to have dessert!"

"No, nothing for me," Laura said.

"Me neither," echoed Tracy.

In the ten seconds of that short exchange, I went from calm and cool to seeing red.

These two twats had to be joking! Here we were in the

restaurant of the Mandalay Bay in Las Vegas, the night after two sold-out shows, and both of them had been gushing all throughout our noontime meal about how amazing the dessert case looked. Foot-high slices of cake, puddings, gelato, and homemade ice cream had distracted all of us throughout our meal, and now that it was time to order, these bitches were punking out.

My head felt like it was about to explode with a mixture of anger, resentment, and betrayal. We were a team, weren't we? We were the *Sex and the City* cast minus the ugly, man-hating dyke one. We were a crew! But now, instead of ordering dessert with me, Tracy and Laura had turned on me, and I hated them for it. At that moment, I knew exactly how a guy feels when a girl invites him back to her apartment and will only give him a dry hump.

"*For-fucking-get it!*" I scream-whispered in that way furious mothers do when they want to yell at their kids in church but don't want the priest to overhear. Fishing in my wallet, I dug out two twenty-dollar bills and threw them on the table. "Enjoy the rest of your fucking day."

Pushing my chair back from the table with a nails-on-chalkboard scratching sound on the tile floor, I stormed out of the restaurant. I'd show those two cunts! They were disloyal and they would see! I steamrolled into my suite and over to my computer to change my flight and get the hell outta there as quickly as I could. And, I vowed, I would never return any of their calls *ever again*.

Hmmm . . . I think I might have overreacted.

Actually, O. J. overreacted.

I overreacted *and* made an ass out of myself.

Well, who could blame me? In the past seven months, I had gotten rid of a no-goodnik of a boyfriend, spent a week in codependency rehab, had two crappy dates, and put a stop to dating yet again. With food the only source of comfort in my life since it was the only thing I could put in my mouth and enjoy, I had gained back almost half the weight I had lost pre-Tommy, and clearly from the exchange in the Vegas restaurant, food was taking on a much more important role in my life than it had a right to. I needed to put a stop to it *now*.

As I sat smoldering in my hotel suite that day, my head pounded from the two-show night before and the angry exchange with my friends. I changed into sweats since they were clothes I felt I could disappear in, and I thought and thought and thought about my food issues.

Clearly, dieting didn't work for me. For more than a quarter-century since my first bout with dieting in my freshman year of college, my weight had gone up and down more than a sorority girl's head on homecoming weekend. That constant cycle of deprive, binge, deprive, binge had done nothing for me except give me a monthlong taste—at the most—of being thin before I gained all the weight back, plus some. It was clear: dieting didn't work. So, what would?

Sitting waiting for the red-eye that night in Vegas, I thought about all the diets that had let me down. There was the five-hundred-calorie-a-day plan from the Diet Center in Boston when I was eighteen. Now, to put this in perspective, five hundred calories is less than the contents of one money shot from a guy who has just been released from jail. That particular slenderizing technique had resulted in a loss of sixty pounds, some of my hair, all of my sex drive, and most of my sanity.

Then there was the eighty-five-pound loss on Weight Watchers right after a graduate program at Harvard, which had stayed off for three months until my dead-end relationship with a former inmate led me to find solace in food once again. And most recently, of course, there was the shedding of thirty pounds on Jenny Craig, which was creeping back up as I sat waiting to board the plane. Now that I think about it, I'm not even sure whether I lost thirty pounds on Jenny Craig or if it just looked like it when I compared myself to Kirstie Alley in the commercials.

Then, as if I was struck by lightning, an idea occurred to me. I had been able to stop contacting Tommy—and dating at all—because I was "feeling my feelings." That's what they had advised us to do in codependency rehab instead of reaching for the phone when we felt lonely, sad, angry, or insecure. So why couldn't I do the same thing with food? I mean, I was obviously eating more than I needed to if the weight was coming back, so what if instead of eating when I felt those same emotions, I simply "felt"? It was worth a try. And since I'd learned how to shed Tommy in codependency rehab, maybe there was a food rehab somewhere out there where I could learn to do the same with food. Although, when I thought about it, food would definitely be harder to shake than Tommy since it smelled better and didn't finish ten minutes before I did.

Too embarrassed by my problem to ask my assistant to do an online search for "fat rehab"—I still hadn't lived down the time I'd asked her to find me a really good set of ass beads that didn't chafe—I whipped out my laptop and went for it. The first place I discovered was Sierra Tucson, a world-renowned addiction facility, which offered a forty-five-day food issues program. Forty-five days! That was longer than Lent. I mean, some murderers do less time in jail! Forty-five days was a lot. I knew I could talk my manager into a month off, but a month and a half would be pushing it. A month and a half off and I'd starve anyway because of the way I like to live and shop.

Continuing on, I found a website for Rosewood Ranch, which offered an intensive in-patient program for seriously obese, bulimic, and anorexic people but also had a partial out-patient program, starting at twenty-eight days—the standard length of a stay in rehab.

Now, that was more like it. I could swing the twenty-eight days. But there was one problem: I was under contract to work for the next four months straight, and as with all addicts, I wanted results *now*! Besides, if I waited to work on my food addiction until June, I would be ten pounds fatter. And if I continued to behave like a crazed wildebeest, the only thing I was going to lose was the friendship of my two petite openers.

Scrolling down the page on which I had Googled "food addiction" and "rehab centers," I spotted an entry for Onsite in Tennessee. Onsite's website said they were a facility with weeklong workshops named things like "Healing Money Issues," "Healing Sexual Issues (Men)," and "Healing Sexual Issues (Women)." I scrolled down their list, past "Living Centered" and "Equine Therapy"—horses? What the fuck?!?—and there it was: "Healing Food Issues." That was me! I had food issues and they could be healed *in five days*—just like my codependency had been healed at Caron. Five days! What a score—it usually took more time than that for my hemorrhoid medication to kick in. Perfect! I had some time off in a month, right before I was scheduled to go to the Grammys, so I decided that this was meant to be! By the end of the next day, I had signed up and booked my ticket to Nashville.

None of the fear and trepidation I had about my first stint in rehab was present as I drove from the Nashville airport to the little town of Cumberland Furnace, Tennessee—well, no fears other than the normal healthy ones associated with any trip to the backwoods of Tennessee. Gone were the anxieties about white-coated orderlies administering electroshock treatments and midnight rapes. Gone were my suspicions that Nurse Ratched would visit me after lights-out for a midnight lesbian cornholing. Nope—instead, as I wound my way to the Onsite campus, I was more worried about the possibility of seeing lawn jockeys in actual black and Confederate flags proudly displayed by people who hadn't evolved past the 1800s. As I found my way through the four or so towns between the airport and my destination, I checked every house with a porch, expecting to see a small retarded boy playing a banjo. But as always seems the case with these rehab facilities, my journey ended at a lovely little farmhouse, but this time, the farmhouse was surrounded by woods and tiny cabins where, I assumed, all the fatties would be staying for the week.

Initially, I thought it was cruel to put fat people in housing that would remind them of their favorite syrup—Log Cabin. I mean, if my roommate ended up being a black woman with a handkerchief around her head, I knew I'd be at Waffle House in half an hour. But it turns out that, unlike the Caron Foundation, Onsite didn't have the ball-busting roommate policy I had hated. I had made sure before I signed up that I would have a room all to myself since I would be attending the Grammys the following week and I couldn't afford to be kept up by potential roommates' snoring or crying. No, I had to be at the top of my game when I spent the disappointing, all-this-effort-for-nothing Grammy weekend in L.A. After hearing me out, the administration at Onsite gave me a private room—at no extra charge! This is, by the way, the one and only perk that being a chubby female celebrity provides. And when I showed up there on that drizzly day in February, I discovered what a room it was!

My cabin was something right out of a magazine ad for a quaint little bed-and-breakfast. After I dragged my two fifty-pound suitcases up the four or five steps to the front door (when these rehab facilities will start employing bellmen, I will *never* know!), I turned the lock and entered the room that would be my home for the next five days. Complete with cute country-chic bedspreads and pillow shams, the room was filled with warmth—figuratively and literally—as the fireplace glowed to greet me. Hoisting my bags onto the spare bed, I slowly unpacked, relishing the aloneness and telling myself how lucky I was to have secured such a peaceful room, all to myself. At that moment, I knew serenity would wash over me for the remainder of my days there.

"IT'S MY SECOND TIME HERE." The female voice came crashing through the wall, interrupting my reverie. I had been lost in my fantasy that the loudest noise I would hear at On-site that week would be the tinkling of delicate copper wind chimes, but the *voice* snapped me back to reality. It was so loud and clear that I hightailed it into the bathroom to see if another patient had taken up residence in my shower.

"I WAS HERE ABOUT EIGHT YEARS AGO FOR THE

LIVING CENTERED PROGRAM," the voice continued. "SO NOW I'M BACK TO WORK ON MY FOOD ISSUES."

Holy crap! This week wasn't going to be awash in the sea of tranquility after all. Seems that my half of the lovely little log cabin was just that—only half the space of the entire house— and on the other side of the flimsiest of plywood walls, a wall thinner than one in a Brazilian slum shanty, there were three women bunking together and each seemed to have the acoustical range of Celine Dion. Like 'Til Tuesday said in the eighties, voices carry.

Oddly though, I wasn't feeling what I normally would have felt under such noisy circumstances: annoyance. Okay, well, I was a *little* annoyed. But mostly, the emotion that surfaced was that of being left out, ignored, and I knew it was just a matter of time before my self-esteem would plummet into "not good enough." At that moment, I decided I needed to knock on that plywood wall and join the party—although Richard Simmons is the only guy I've ever heard of who thought four chunky bitches working on their weight issues was a "party."

"Uh, I just wanted to let you guys know that I can hear everything you say." I searched to find the right words to convey what I was trying to tell my housemates, Charlotte, Karen, and Vanessa. "I mean, not that it was disturbing me—I have earplugs. I just wanted you to know that if there's something you don't want me to hear, it's only fair you know that these walls are thin."

Just like the three good little codependents they were, the ladies couldn't apologize quickly or vehemently enough. Truth be told, they had nothing to apologize about. I actually enjoy eavesdropping, but since the place ran on confidentiality, I thought I better go introduce myself before I ripped a loud one and they knew I could hear them too.

Karen interrupted my stammering by grabbing a chair, bringing it over to me, and insisting I get out of the door frame and sit down. The eldest of the group, Karen, from that moment on, was the mom of the group—the self-aware, willing-to-work-on-herself mom none of us had ever had. Instantly put at ease, I chatted with them until it was meal-time—the only group activity none of us ever seemed to want to be late for.

Strolling over to the main building where meals were pre-pared and eaten, we learned that each group ate in a separate room, depending on its issues. We food addicts ate in a room near the front of the house that was decorated entirely in antiques with tons of doilies and nothing whatsoever edible. No fruit. No little candies. No scented candles. Nothing. Coincidentally—or possibly *not* coincidentally—this was the coldest room in the main building, plus it was the room far-thest from the buffet line. I guess their thinking was that if we wanted food so badly, we wouldn't mind the walk. And we were the ones who were sufficiently bulked up to handle a chill.

In the room across the hall from us was the group of folks working on their money issues; the counselors ate in the room next to us; and lastly, toward the back of the house and right near the buffet was the mysterious group with the door closed, the guys working on their sexual issues.

As we split up to eat in our assigned rooms, we closed the door and the gossip began. Joining the three girls and me in the food issues group was one male, and I instantly knew two things about him upon saying hello: He was gayer than Siegfried and Roy's tigers, and he had recognized me instantly. Where the three women weren't in on my identity, Kyle's combination of being chubby and gay put him smack in the middle of my comedy target demographic. I don't know why I was surprised to meet someone like him at Onsite. We were in the woods—I was bound to run into a bear. From the second I met him, I knew Kyle would be my partner in crime at Onsite, and by "partner," I mean someone with whom I could check out all the hot sex addicts.

But, it turns out, this wasn't going to be as easy as it seemed. While the "Healing Sexual Issues" guys dined near us, did their group therapy near us, and ate snacks in the communal kitchen around the same time as us, not one of them would acknowledge us. And I'll admit it, after day two, my self-esteem was at an all-time low. I mean, here were guys who, I assumed, would jump on the ground and fuck a crack in the sidewalk, and I couldn't get even one to look at me.

Now, looking back, I know this way of thinking was horrible. Hoping to have sex with a guy working on sexual addiction would be the equivalent of one of them hoping to get me to eat a Twinkie. However, based on the fact that I would have killed for a Twinkie, I figured at least I had a shot.

I stopped wearing sweats and started wearing my cute camouflage pants and pink tops, and did my hair and makeup every day—not the full treatment, but the "I'm not trying hard 'cause I'm in rehab, but I'm still cute" look. I *knew* I had to be at least one of the fifteen guys' type! There was a super-hot black guy, a couple of Latinos, and a few very rough-trade-looking white guys. At least one of them should have found me slightly adorable.

And as part of the chubby group, I knew I would be the one they would notice first. Karen was too old for them and was a mother figure; Charlotte was *way* too classy with her gorgeous Southern accent and artistic sensibility; Vanessa was married and made sure everybody knew it; and Kyle was a big fuckin' fag. I was the easy mark, goddamn it! There was no lock on my panties and they definitely didn't have to solve a riddle to get into my vagina!

But no matter how hard I tried, no matter how many times I timed my visits to the kitchen to coincide with my prime targets', I got nothing more than a nod before the object of my desire beat a hasty retreat. I didn't know what to do! I was trying to work on my food issues, so I couldn't eat through the terrible feelings this was bringing up for me. I couldn't drown my sorrows in male attention, since I couldn't get any of the straight guys to throw me even a hello. So I had nothing to do but face my feelings—the entire point of rehab. Sadly, I wanted to do anything but that.

In my room one afternoon after another ignored-by-sex-addicts morning, I scrolled through the contact list in my phone. Yeah, I know what you're thinking—aren't you supposed to hand in your phone when you check in? Yes, assholes. But I had told the powers that be at Onsite that due to my Grammy nomination—i.e., supreme importance—I had to be in possession of the phone at all times. However, I had promised to only check it once a day, and I had vowed to never, *ever* use it to dial evil ex-boyfriends and people who triggered my food issues.

Scanning the list of contacts in my phone, I made a list of
people who were not technically in those categories. There
was Jerry in Chicago—my pre-Tommy boyfriend who had
become a friend with flirting privileges. There was Derrick
in Minneapolis, a very hot Denzel lookalike who was a fireman I was planning to hook up with in a month. And there
was Charlie, a light-skinned chubby fan with a heroin-addict
brother, who I liked to talk recovery with. So I planned it
out—any time the feelings became too much and I couldn't
pick up food or one of the sex addicts, I could text or call one
of them and make the pain go away.

Yes, I know, I know—I should have been journaling, reading, working on my issues. But, at the time, I guess you could
say I just wasn't ready. If I needed a "harmless" conversation
with a man to get through the week, so be it. And even though
this would distract me from working on myself, the seminar
was only a little over $2,000, plus airfare. Even if it was a
waste of time, I could make that money back in my next seven
minutes onstage.

One day after lunch, I realized I had about thirty minutes
until our next therapy group and headed into my cabin under
the guise of taking a nap. Since our days always began around
six thirty A.M. with morning meditation—what a *load!*—
everyone was usually exhausted by noon. Locking the door, I
texted my black fireman and his response was instant.

"I was on the news last night, boo," he typed.

"What for?" I queried.

"Put out a fire at the news station. Wanna see a picture?"

You bet I did. First of all, as everyone knows, firemen are

hot. Second, black firemen are even hotter. There's something really sexy about watching a black man run into a building instead of out of it with a plasma TV under his arm.

And what a picture it was! There was my hero, in his gear, posing for a photo on his triumphant evening of saving lives. Well, that was all it took to get my motor running. I knew I had to take care of this need now. I saved the photo and hopped to it.

My excitement was nearly quelled when I realized my situation. Here I was, ragingly horny for the first time since I had come to Onsite, but surveying the room, I realized that getting the job done here was going to be tougher than I thought. First of all, it was daylight and everyone was walking around the grounds. I ran to the windows, hoping to pull the curtains shut, but when I did, I noticed they were so sheer, so transparent, that anyone could see in them without even squinting.

Now that I think about it, the curtains were probably flimsy so the sex addicts wouldn't spend their every waking moment jerking off. In fact, I had heard that the sex addicts were required to sign a contract saying they wouldn't spank it the entire week they were there. But I wasn't a sex addict! I was just fucking fat! I deserved real curtains! Besides, no one wants to see a fat bitch rocking the little man in the boat by herself.

With only seventeen minutes left before group, I raced into the bathroom, the only windowless room in the place. Instantly hearing voices from the adjoining room, I realized that if I could hear them, they would certainly be able to hear me, and I couldn't risk them hearing my solo action. And since the bathroom was divided into two tiny rooms, there was no place to even sit down and get comfortable and make the magic happen.

By then, I was hotter than ever and determined to make it work. Kicking the door shut between the two parts of the bathroom, I turned on both the sink and the shower to drown out any noise I might make. I considered lying in the bathtub but would never have had time to do my hair and makeup again on the off chance one of the sex addicts would say hello to me. So, wedging my five-foot-nine frame into the four-foot space on the floor in front of the bathtub, I propped my feet up against the door at a forty-five-degree angle and did the same on the opposite wall with my neck and shoulders. In short, at that angle I looked like a partially opened Swiss Army knife and it was anything but comfortable, sexy, or romantic.

Now, believe me, I'm quick—in fact, I often finish faster than my partners. But today, with my neck crooked and my feet up against the door in case any staff member should let himself in for a random room check, I was taking more time than usual. Plus, now I was starting to break a sweat since the only thermostat was in the girls' room and for some reason those bitches had it cranked up to a hundred. And my neck, which hadn't been the same since a car accident when I was thirty, was starting to throb from the uncomfortable position it held on the wood-paneled wall. "Holy crap," I thought, "how do people in trailer parks do it?!?" This clearly wasn't going to be my best effort. But I was gonna finish, goddamn it! I hadn't come this far not to come!

With only three minutes left to spare, I was finally done. Flushed and even more exhausted than when I had gone into my room for my "nap," I jogged over to the main building for group therapy.

"Did you have a good rest?" Charlotte asked sweetly as I came in.

"Oh, yeah, great," I responded, my eyes quickly darting up and to the left—a sure sign that I was telling a little white lie.

"Hmmm," I thought. "Note to self: Sign up for 'Healing Sexual Issues' workshop asap."

CHAPTER ELEVEN

Porkers, Pukers, and Purgers

hree months later, it was May 20, 2008—a mere three days after my sold-out show at Carnegie Hall, perhaps the most impressive concert venue in the United States, if not the world. Actually, when you're a comic, any venue whose name doesn't include the word "chuckle" or "hut" feels like a step up. But three days later, my location was a far cry from Carnegie Hall's revered vaulted ceilings. I was in a room with three walls made of cinder block and one of bad pine paneling straight out of the Brady Bunch's basement. I was lying on a hard mattress—

not hard in the "it's good for my lower back" kind of way, but hard in the "belongs in a hotel that charges by the hour" kind of way—and I was staring at a three-inch-thick binder of rules, mealtimes, and twelve-step worksheets. My suitcases had been searched, my car keys had been taken away, and my door could be opened at any time by any staff member without any notice. It was like being a teenager under my mother's roof all over again.

I was in rehab for the third time in a year. I was a reality show and two fits of 'roid rage away from being Danny Bonaduce. And these were the walls I would stare at for the next twenty-eight days.

Unfortunately, after my one week in codependency rehab and my five-day food issues workshop, I knew I needed more. Having spent the better part of both those weeks making friends and figuring out how to squeeze one off, I knew a longer, more hard-core stint in rehab was needed. I'd had food issues ever since I came out of the womb, and they weren't going to get resolved in a week. I needed to commit myself the way people who needed to kick heroin committed themselves. So, after watching Sandra Bullock's movie *28 Days*, I told my manager that I would be taking May 19 through June 17 to work on myself. Right after Carnegie Hall, I was going to rehab for the third, and I hoped final, time.

As I write this, I have to admit to myself and to you, dear reader, that this decision wasn't exactly easy. I had had enough glimmers of hope on the outside that made me want to take that month and spend it like normal people spend their vacation—getting sunburned at the beach and arguing with my friends and family. I was long done with Tommy, I wasn't dating and indeed felt more complete than ever without men, and I wasn't excessively overeating. I had a new shrink and I was going to several types of weekly twelve-step meetings. I even had a sponsor who was helping me work Step 1, which is admitting I am powerless over food. Oh, I was powerless all right. I had found it impossible to tell the Pillsbury Dough-boy no.

But now, things were different. I was working on it. I told my shrink I didn't need the twenty-eight-day program. I was starting to feel better about myself and I could use the $18,000 the rehab would cost for charity. (Prada's a nonprofit, right?) I had stopped gaining weight and had found some cute summer clothes in size XXL at Target. Who knew they even carried that size, except for the black women on TV's *Big Ass Barbecue*?

Then something happened that made me say yes to rehab again. I'll call it Hurricane Bubba.

Now, those of you who know me know I have an uncanny connection with Sirius Satellite Radio's Bubba the Love Sponge. For some reason, Bubba gets an unusually large kick out of me, and I am hugely tickled by him. In fact, Sirius program director Tim Sabean has told me on more than one occasion that if there's one woman who can hold her own with the more-demented-than-Stern Bubba, it's me. Our on-air chemistry is magic, and due to the genuine warmth we have for each other, a friendship had developed effortlessly between us.

I have always looked forward to appearing on Bubba's show—especially in person—and looking at my calendar, I realized that shortly after the Grammys, I would be in Florida with my brother's family. That meant I could drive over and do an in-person appearance on Bubba's show in a few short hours. I suggested this to Bubba's producer, Spice Boy, and Bubba was thrilled since we hadn't seen each other in over a year, when I had appeared in-studio with Tommy. So it was settled that right after Disney World with the family, I would drive to Tampa and hang out on the show. I couldn't stop smiling thinking about chilling with my radio pal.

But then it was the night before the show, and I stopped smiling. That's because I looked in my suitcase and found that none of my outfits seemed to fit.

Having lost thirty pounds on my pre-Tommy Jenny Craig diet—and loving the *mucho atención* I'd gotten for my new look from Howard Stern, Bubba, and every other radio and TV host the previous year—I had been on a high. But my weight had gone up fifteen pounds since then, and I was not only looking fuller around the thighs, middle, and stomach area, I was in a panic. Every time someone asked me if I was keeping my weight off, I assured them I was. Surely they couldn't tell I was gaining the weight back. I was doing my best to cover up my weight gain with my vast assortment of pants with built-in Spanx slimmers, suck-in camisoles, and corsets, which is basically the fat girl's equivalent of the comb-over. But the night before Bubba, I was in a sweat, and it wasn't the Florida heat or the three-alarm dump I'd taken because of the hot wings I'd eaten. I had packed fourteen—no lie, fourteen—potential outfits for Bubba's show, and as I tore them off the hangers, I realized that the truth about me and my weight gain would be discovered and I would be humiliated on national radio. If Bubba was televised, I probably would have shot myself right then and there.

"So what?" you might say. "It's fifteen pounds. Big deal." So this, folks. It *was* a big deal. Food addicts are just that—*addicts*. We sneak food, we hide food, we try to camouflage our extra poundage with undergarments, and we generally blanch at the idea of people discovering our dirty little secret, much like a heroin addict hides his habit. We don't shoot smack between our toes—we stuff Twinkies down our pie hole when no one is looking. Now, of course, the two problems are very different—heroin can kill you tomorrow and the food will take a while longer. But either way, both addictions are surrounded with shame at our failings and the feeling of not being good enough.

That night before Bubba, I was so panic stricken at the thought of him finding out about my addiction that I knew I never wanted to feel that way again. The shame at gaining weight was so overwhelming I called every person I knew from Overeaters Anonymous—I even bothered my shrink at home at eleven P.M. (yes, those are billable hours)—and after many tears and near hyperventilation, I came up with a plan.

I would do what all women do in a time of crisis—I would use my tits. Oh, bitches, don't kid yourselves. We are our boobs! Whether it's Mardi Gras, a screaming baby, or a frustrated second date, all a woman needs to soothe the savage beast is some breasts. So I would show off my rack, hopefully distract Bubba from my expanded waist, and if by some chance he were to mention my weight gain, I would cop to it. I would then divert the discussion with my humor and deflect the ensuing insults onto him, since he had also gained quite a few pounds. I would end the discussion by saying I was going to fat rehab and then, when I came back the next time, the fifteen pounds would be melted off. I hoped.

If that didn't work, I would rip one during the commercial, blame him, and leave.

Well, the gods were on my side that day. Either that, or Bubba's eyes were so clouded with friendship for me that he mentioned nothing about my appearance except—you guessed it—*boobs*. He commented on them several times, and even when we both stood side by side to take photos, he called me "skinny," a feat I accomplished with my flouncy, low-cut blouse and a Gucci messenger bag strategically placed across my middle to hide the spread that wasn't there the year before. I had escaped unscathed! My secret was safe. Now, if I could just get through my next Stern appearance in May, and then my next Bubba appearance in August, and then Stern again in September, I didn't need rehab, right?

Bouncing, quite literally, into my shrink's office the week after my triumphant Bubba appearance, I was elated. "I did it—the show was great," I announced to the doctor, who looked at me skeptically but not judgmentally. "He didn't notice I gained weight, so my secret's safe. I don't think I need rehab. I mean, Bubba's really critical, and if he didn't say anything, I don't have to go. It's not like I bottomed out or something."

The doctor gazed at me and in a calm voice said, "So, you don't think calling everyone you know hysterically crying the night before the show was bottoming out? Carrying fourteen outfits that you're afraid to try on all the way to Florida isn't bottoming out? You don't think all the shame you're carrying and the secret you're keeping is bottoming out? Sounds like bottoming out to me."

Maybe the doctor was right. I *had* called him in the middle of the night, effectively ruining any shot he had of hitting it with his wife. I *had* paid $150 in extra baggage charges to bring over a dozen outfits for a *non-televised* show. And I *had* been terrified of the opinion of someone who refers to himself as a "love sponge." Something was definitely wrong.

Reluctantly, I had no choice but to agree with him. It sounded like bottoming out to me too. Later that day, I booked my twenty-eight-day reservation at Rosewood Ranch. Good-bye vacation, hello hard work.

A month later, as I drove the two hundred miles from the Tucson airport to the little one-horse/plethora-of-rehabs town of Wickenburg, Arizona, I was boiling hot but not too scared. The only people who knew where I was going were my manager, my best friends, my group of three "food issues" friends from Onsite, and my assistant, who was instructed not to call or e-mail me unless it was a life-or-death emergency. I had told my parents I was going to my house at Canyon Ranch health spa for a month so they wouldn't worry about me, since they had seen my place and, after falling in love with it, had agreed that it was a great environment for me to decompress in. I figured it would be easier for them to have a good month if they pictured me getting massages, playing tennis, laying by the pool, and taking yoga classes, rather than imagining me spending sixteen hours a day in twelve-step meetings and group therapy that would ultimately paint them as the bad guys. Some would call this deceiving them, others would call it protecting them. Either way, I figured, no harm, no foul. What they didn't know wouldn't hurt them, and my twenty-eight days exploring my past could only help our relationship when I got sprung. Besides, I was a forty-six-year-old adult. I was allowed to have a few secrets, wasn't I? In fact, after I told them I was dating the blacks, I figured the more secrets the better.

The drive was pleasant enough, thanks to the air-conditioning in my Toyota, but when I got out of the car to get gas, the dry Arizona heat hit me like a wall. I was wearing what I considered a summer outfit, a sundress from Target, which might have been comfortable in the dense heat had it not been for the black tights and three-quarter-length-sleeve thermal shirt I wore underneath. Let me explain.

Summer is the chubby/fat girl's least favorite time of the year—and not just for the obvious bathing suit traumas every girl, even the skinny ones, experiences. It is physically impossible for chubby girls to wear summer clothes, look good, and stay cool. This is because of our several problem areas. The first problem area for me has always been my generous ass and thighs. Wear a summer dress with nothing but panties, and what do you get? Jiggling. And to a fat girl, nothing feels worse than the real or imagined wiggle-waggle as she walks down, say, the boardwalk, ice cream cone in hand. Just thinking about it, I had a flashback to the old Jell-O commercial "Watch it wiggle, see it jiggle." Fat girl solution? Add a pair of black Spanx footless tights, which, sure, look cute and reduce the involuntary ass movement, but unfortunately add about twenty degrees to the overall body temperature. And isn't that what every guy wants? A cute girl with a tight body who can't stop sweating?

Then there was the three-quarter-sleeve thermal shirt. No self-respecting plump princess will bare her arms above the elbows under penalty of death. The underarm flab where the tricep should be—the "bingo arm," as we in the Catholic

Church like to call it—plus the cottage cheese cellulite must be hidden under an adorable top, even if it cuts off the circulation in the elbow with elastic so tight it makes the joint ache.

But the important thing was I showed up to fat rehab looking decent. I wouldn't want the other food addicts to think they were cuter than me.

So, as I drove nearer to the town that would be my home for nearly a month, I was certainly sweaty, but at least I wasn't petrified. I'd gotten through two places like this before and I could do it again.

Rosewood Ranch's Capri Campus looks like any other run-down roadside drive-up motel weary travelers stop at to grab a quick night's sleep and a lukewarm shower before heading on to a finer destination like Prescott, Phoenix, or even the oxymoronically named Surprise, Arizona. But instead of low-budget RVers and families of wandering Mexicans inside its walls, on any given week, Rosewood Capri houses anywhere from a dozen to twenty-one women with food issues, most of them recently released from Rosewood's medically staffed main building (Rosewood Ranch) a few miles away.

There are huge differences between Rosewood Ranch and the Capri Campus. Most interesting to me, of course, was the fact that at Capri, patients are allowed to flush their own toilets. You see, since many of the patients at the Ranch are bulimics and anorexics who tend to hate eating and love throwing up and/or pooping using laxatives, even bowel movements are supervised. Many of the patients at Rosewood—affectionately nicknamed by the girls "Porkers, Pukers, and Purgers"—entered the facility on death's doorstep, and to its credit, Rosewood has saved hundreds, if not thousands, of lives. If I ever had a daughter who was a porker, puker, or purger, she'd be on the next train to Rosewood. Well, right after we finished auditioning her for Disney's *High School Musical 4*.

That being said, even on Rosewood's Capri Campus—the facility's partial hospitalization program—there are lots of rules. Sure, there might not be the nurse around every corner, the pooping with the door open, or the absence of patients' cell phones and laptops. But there are rules nonetheless. There's no Sweet'N Low (which is both an artificial sweetener *and* my nickname for my snatch), no other sugar substitutes, nor any diet foods (these foods can cause inaccurate hunger signals and reinforcement of the "diet" mentality—very bad). There is absolutely no caffeine, a substance that causes an artificial high, therefore getting in the way of the purpose of Rosewood's therapy, i.e., feeling your feelings. And all meals are eaten together.

Now, sure, this might be fun if Capri consisted of twenty fat women sitting around a table chowing down. However, when I entered the facility, I was surprised to find very few fat chicks—about three, myself included. The rest were fifteen women who ranged from delightfully shaped to rail thin to Darfur skeletons. Now, usually, I don't mind eating with skinny women. But that was on the outside, where there was no rule against eating off of their plates. Eating with the thin women of Rosewood wasn't gonna be the blast it was in the real world. But I didn't know how miserable it was going to be until two hours after arrival on my first day there.

After having my bags searched and looted by a lovely lesbian yoga specialist called Summer, I watched her exit my room with two boxes of my Jenny Craig Anytime bars, about ninety-five packets of Sweet'N Low, all my breath mints ("They have sugar substitute, you know?"), and nine packages of my Dentyne Ice. I couldn't help thinking that Summer looked disappointed that she hadn't found anything more contraband in my bags. There was no Ex-Lax (I had tried laxatives once in college but stopped after one day when I spent three hours on the shitter), no drugs (vitamins have always been the only pills in my repertoire), and no alcohol (the few times I'd gotten drunk in my lifetime, I'd suffered too much with hangovers to consider making it a habit).

As I unpacked, I scanned the room that I would sleep in for the next month. It sure wasn't the Four Seasons, but it could have been worse. There was an in-the-wall air-conditioning unit that kept the Arizona heat at bay, a small desk for my laptop, and lots of drawer space for the ton of clothes and toiletries I figured I needed for my stay. To top it off, I, unlike everyone else at Capri, once again, had managed to get myself a private room in rehab. Having explained to the intake manager my huge fame and celebrity status, hence my need for privacy, I was allowed to have a room to myself, for an extra three grand. To me, this was money well spent.

As I killed some time setting up my laptop, I heard a key in the lock, and Summer popped her head in. "Carole needs to see you."

Taken aback by someone unlocking and entering my room without knocking, I said, "I'm not doing anything," as guiltily as if I'd been checking out hotanorexics.com, and shut the laptop. She said, "No problem," and escorted me to the office of Carole, the nutritionist, who would soon become my favorite person at Rosewood.

Unlike all the super-skinny dieticians I've seen over the years, Carole was what I like to call "normal size." She was a woman who I assessed to be about a size 12 on the top and a 14 on the bottom, and she seemed completely unfazed by it. Her warm personality and huge knowledge base were going to prove my salvation in the next few weeks, and our first meeting was no different. We chatted easily about my dieting history and my goals (to stop emotional eating and, "if it was meant to be," to drop a few pounds, like maybe the fifteen or so I'd gained in the past year). I told Carole I had never been bulimic, I had never been anorexic, but I held a lifetime achievement award for compulsive eating. Then Carole weighed me but refused to tell me the number. When I asked her why, Carole explained that women with food issues are too focused on the number of pounds they weigh, so the staff keeps that to themselves. That made sense. I guess weight to a woman is kind of like what penis size is to a man—we hang our self-esteem on it, and once you've seen a disappointing figure, you can't think about anything else. Then she escorted me through the main meeting room and into the kitchen, where the girls were sitting down to eat dinner.

"Bridget, this is Lisa. She's new. Please show her how to eat," Carole told a beautiful young girl dressed in tights, tall boots, a tie-dyed shirt, and a pixie haircut. "I know how to eat," I thought as I stared at Carole and this little Peter Pan–looking, twenty-year-old hippie. "I know how to eat a little too well. Why the fuck else would I be here?"

Consulting the food plan Carole had written up for me, Bridget showed me how to measure out the meal that had been cooked that evening by the girls for communal consumption. I was allowed three proteins, two starches, one vegetable, one fruit, and one fat—translation, "Boy, am I glad I stopped at Wendy's on the way here."

As I sat down with my paltry amount of food, some of the girls greeted me, others were too overwrought at forcing their "huge" portions down to say hello, and still others just ate slowly. I kept my part of the conversation to safe subjects like where I was from, how my flight and drive were, and the weather. I had to keep my dinner conversation innocuous since I had received the "Common Food Rituals" sheet a few hours before and was scared to break any of the huge list of don'ts for mealtimes at Rosewood.

The list was longer than the Ten Commandments and the twelve steps combined. In small part, it read:

1.   No focusing on the food behaviors of peers. For example, my usual commenting on other people's food intake, like "You're really gonna eat all that?" or "C'mon, skin-n-bones! That steak ain't gonna eat and throw itself up" would not be welcome here.

2.   *No cutting crust off of bread.* Apparently, grade school kids have a lot of food issues.

3.   *No pulling sandwiches apart or eating them with silverware.* I had no idea what harm that could do, unless being pretentious interferes with your treatment.

4.   *No letting food "slip" to the floor.* And, in my case, no pretending to tie your shoe so you can eat it.

5. *No hiding food, or spitting out food into napkins.* I thought they should add a rule saying we couldn't stuff vegetables down our pants, but that's for a whole different reason.

6. *No excessive fluid intake and no ice in milk.* Who the fuck puts ice in milk? The only thing I want to stick in milk is a cookie.

7. *No mixing foods together inappropriately.* Cripes! If the people at Reese's had attended rehab at Rosewood, the peanut butter cup would never have been invented.

8. *No smacking lips, making noises, grunts, or groans. No excessive talking during meals. No discussion of calories, fat, or meal plans, and no talk involving profanity or violence.* Man, my family would have never lasted through one meal at Rosewood!

As I was devouring the last of my carefully counted out seventeen red grapes, one of the girls said, "Okay, I'll start." What she meant was she would begin what Rosewood refers to as "meal processing," a mandatory ritual that takes place after every meal.

"Okay, I was in at a three and out at a seven. I am exactly where God wants me to be. I love my body."

Fuckin' what!!!!???!!!!

The next girl, a far chunkier one at the head of the table, piped up. "I was in at a four, out at a six. I am a patient and tolerant woman. I am a patient and tolerant woman."

I had no idea what these bitches were talking about. And

they were going around the table, and it was closing in on me. I was positively tongue-tied—can you imagine *that*?!? Me? At a loss for words? I looked around desperately, but there weren't even any minorities to make fun of. (I guess minorities can't afford the eighteen grand.)

The girl across from me sensed my confusion and said, "We go around and use the hunger scale to say how hungry we were when the meal started and how full we are when the meal ends. Then we give two positive affirmations about ourselves—if you can't think of two, you can repeat the same one twice."

Riffling through my white Rosewood binder, I found the hunger scale handout. When it was my turn, I began:

"All right. I was in at a three [definition: You can definitely eat, but you are not on the verge of collapse] and I'm out at a five [You are not hungry anymore. Your body has what it needs and is satisfied]."

I searched my head for an affirmation, maybe something I'd heard in a meeting or while reading one of the dozens of self-help books I bought, read four pages of, and relegated to a box marked "Self-Help Books, Second String." Then I scanned my act for a comment but remembered the "no profanity" rule. Apparently, saying "I am beloved by the fags" would be out of the question.

Instead, I said, "Um, I, uh, I can do this." The girls nodded their assent, visibly appreciating my positive first-day newbie attitude. "And, uh, I can do this one *meal* at a time."

"Ahh"s and knowing looks ricocheted back at me. Obviously, I had impressed the girls with my adaptation of the twelve-step saying "One day at a time" to jive with our current situation. As the last girl spoke, a cry went up through the group: "Rosewood cheer!"

Dismayed, I looked around as a clapping was heard throughout the room and the mealtime cheer went up:

> *I* [clap, clap]
> *Do what it takes* [clap, clap]
> *I persevere* [clap, clap]
> *I am worthwhile* [clap, clap]
> *I face my fear, whooo!!!*
> *Boogety-boogety-boogety, growl!*
> *Gotta do it, gotta do it, gotta do it, do it, do it! Cha-chow!*

The only line that was missing from the cheer was:

> *Patty cake, patty cake, I want some fucking cake!*

A cheer?!? If saying *that* wouldn't kill my desire to eat, nothing would.

As the group cleared their dishes away, I tried to hide my apprehension for this crazy, cheerleadery fat camp by looking over the hunger scale in the binder. My stomach growled as I leafed through the literature. With the minuscule amount I was allowed to eat at each meal, I wondered if it would ever be possible to be out at an eight (You feel as if they are going to have to put you on a truck and haul you away. Your body is screaming, "Get me out of here!").

I knew my body might never scream that at Rosewood, but my mind was just about there already.

CHAPTER TWELVE

Escape from Wickenburg

"No apologies allowed! If I apologize, call me on it!"

I looked down at the pink tattered sign that was held around my neck with a fraying piece of lavender yarn. I had slipped it over my head nearly twenty-four hours before, and it was finally almost time for it to come off.

You see, in rehab—even food rehab—you do as you're told. And what I had been told yesterday by my therapist Dee was that I apologize too much. I apologize for my opinions, I apologize for my feelings, I even apologize when I know the other person is clearly wrong. So, when she heard me in group saying, "I'm sorry, I just feel like I'm weak for having this issue. I mean, I haven't learned anything in forty-eight years. Never mind—forget I said anything. I'm sorry," she glanced around the room at the seven other girls in the circle.

"You know what I think Lisa needs?" Dee said, already knowing what the response would be. I made a mental list. A man? A Grammy? A hot fudge sundae? "No apologizing," the girls said in unison with the precision and timing reserved for the Israeli military, Muslim extremists, or the Radio City Rockettes. And before I knew it, I was making a sign that said if anyone caught me apologizing *in any way,* they should bring it to my attention.

Of course, the voice of Lisa Lampanelli, the Queen of Mean, was screaming in my head: "A sign!?! A fucking sign!?! I ain't wearing no sign. Who does she think she is trying to make me wear a sign? Bill Engvall?" But plain ol' Lisa Lampanelli, the chick desperate for a solution to her issues, obediently went down to the crafts table, got out the markers, and did what she was told. Why? Because in rehab, you better surrender or why are you even freakin' there?

"Now, whatever they ask you to do, do it," my therapist in Connecticut had told me the day before I was to depart for Rosewood. "No matter how stupid you think it sounds, whether it's blindfolding you, working with the horses, art therapy . . . just do it. You may not understand the point of it at the time, but no matter how wacky it sounds, there's a reason. Hey, they've got your money. You might as well play along."

And damned if my shrink hadn't been right! For twenty-eight completely exhausting five-A.M.-to-ten-P.M. days packed full of therapy, meetings, and planned meals, half the shit we did sounded like it was straight out of a movie parody. But you know what? As goofy as each individual assignment sounded on paper, as the days went by, I noticed that I was craving sugar less and less, and I was starting to learn about what really makes me tick. Most important, I was feeling my feelings—I had no other choice. With the food cupboard locked and my phone completely empty of men, there was nothing to distract me and help me push down my feelings. I was forced, for the first time in forty-eight years, to focus on me, just like the folks on *Celebrity Rehab with Dr. Drew.*

You ever see that show on VH1? Don't worry, I already know the answer—*no*! Of course you don't watch it, 'cause if you *did* watch it, you wouldn't be reading this book—you'd be watching *Celeb Rehab* and only *Celeb Rehab* on an endless loop day and freakin' night. Yeah, folks—it's *that* fucking good! It's like all those other horrible has-been reality shows, only in this one, the participants actually pretend to want the help they so obviously need.

And you know what? *Celebrity Rehab* is no exaggeration. Sure, there are cameras and losers who do the show for all the wrong reasons, but it really *is* a true representation of how it is in the real joint. During my month in Rosewood working on my food issues, I could have cast that show twenty times over. We had our own Jeff Conaway, a lovable but doped-up older broad whose self-esteem was the only thing that hung lower than her tits. There was our own Mary Carey, who wowed us with stories of sucking dick in plain sight on a dance floor and having so many abortions her story changed every time we heard it. Put it this way: This chick had so many abortions, she got one free with her Planned Parenthood punch card. And then there was me—the gregarious, not-quite-as-tall and not-quite-as-crazy Brigitte Nielsen who added some fun to the group.

And trust me, injecting some levity into this group wasn't easy. Every morning at five A.M., the alarm would go off and I'd shake my head, asking myself the Pet Shop Boys' eternal question, "What have I, what have I, what have I done to deserve this?" But before my feet hit the floor, I'd quickly remind myself that it would be worth all the early mornings, twelve-step meetings, and tearful sessions in group therapy if I could just stop eating and dating to medicate myself. All I had to do was think back to my miserable, unmanageable days before I had arrived, and I knew why I was there.

But before you think I went entirely touchy-feely on you, worry not, my fans. I showed little glimmers of being the Lisa Lampanelli you know and love throughout my month there. Hey, I wouldn't be L.L. if I didn't.

❖

"Today, we are going to write a greeting card to Ed," said Honor, the art therapist. (She swears that's her real name, so I have no choice but to believe her, but oh, c'mon!)

"Who," you may ask, "is Ed?" Ed, I was to find out my second day there, was ED, or "eating disorder." Apparently, our eating disorder was so enmeshed in our lives, we not only had a first name for it, it was a *guy's* first name to boot.

"Now, in your card, say good-bye to Ed," Honor said. "As of today, Ed is no longer a part of your life. But since you have shared time with him—some good times and some bad—you need to say good-bye." Of course, I would have preferred to have one last fling with Ed—a "pity binge," so to speak. And I bet he would have too. C'mon, we all know guys hate getting cards.

I looked at the table full of markers, construction paper, crayons, beads, feathers, and other kindergarten arts and crafts essentials and resisted the urge to tell her to stick a brush up her ass and paint with her leather Cheerio. I thought, "I have an eating disorder, ho. I'm not in the special needs class."

Just then, my home shrink's voice in my head echoed the familiar phrase "Do whatever they ask you to." I picked up a brown sheet of construction paper and a dark blue crayon and began to draw for the first time in forty-two years—unless you count penis doodling in library books.

When it was time for us to share our cards, many of the girls' creations were greeted with knowing nods, sympathetic eyes, and tears. When they finally got to me, I knew the group could use a laugh, and I delivered.

On the front of my card was a crude drawing of my face, round with pink-streaked extensions made of feathers. The mouth was open, emitting a cartoon bubble full of the symbols for cursing—"&%$#@?"

"Hey, Ed! In case I haven't been clear . . . ," I read from the front of the card, holding for the laugh I would receive at the punch line inside.

". . . You're the reason God created the word 'Cunt'! Now, step off!! Douchecock!!"

I held up the open card so the rest of the girls could see my standard "XOXO, Lisa Lampl" signature at the bottom.

Now, I realize that this wasn't my finest work. However,

when you're in rehab, it don't take much to add a little humor to such a grave environment. Add to that the fact that I *did* break the "cunt" barrier. So, just as I'd planned it, a huge involuntary laugh came up from all the girls in the group. Even the new girl who had the distended stomach of a starving Ethiopian and the rotting teeth of Beetlejuice emitted a chuckle. And with that, I had a new addiction—I had gotten a laugh in rehab. And it was with a tough crowd of girls whose emotional range hovered between miserable and suicidal about 90 percent of the time. I was hooked.

At the break, I walked outside to the smoking pit. Now, I'm not a smoker—except a good cigar every now and again after a show, at a Friars Club event, or as a home remedy for a yeast infection. But as everyone who's gotten as far as high school knows, the cool kids are always the smokers. That's an inarguable fact. So, every day, during our breaks, I would rush through my food to go hang out with the cool group while they smoked. In fact, it's well known that a lot of the best work people do in rehab happens without therapists, and that is especially true in the smoking pit.

"I know who you are."

The words came from behind me and I turned around.

"I saw you on the roasts, dude. But don't worry, I won't tell anybody," said a tall, lean girl with pin-straight corn silk hair as she exhaled her Camel Light. "If I send you a friend request on MySpace, will you accept me as a friend?"

Now, I'm a nice person. Of course, I'd accept her as my MySpace friend. That's what MySpace is for—pretending to like people. Oh, c'mon! You don't get more than fifty thousand friends by being picky. And as far as her not telling people who I was, I wanted to yell, "Tell people, bitch! You think I've worked my ass off for seventeen years to be anonymous?" But my overall feeling was: "What a rush!!" This chick knew who I was! In Rosewood, I might not have food or men, but I still had my fame, even if it was just from one smirky seventeen-year-old anorexic. But, as I believe is true in anything and especially comedy, all you need is one person who believes. Standing there with my one link to my pre-rehab self, I knew I could build on that and be the star of the place. Trust me, I'm the queen of self-promotion. I would make it my mission to make that happen.

"Just don't be too funny," Meghan interrupted my thoughts as she took a drag off her cigarette. "They made Greer go forty-eight hours without making a joke. They know humor is a defense and a way of avoiding your feelings." And, she left out, a really good way to make a living.

Just as Meghan predicted, the hammer eventually came down. Dee, my therapist, told me I was not allowed to be funny for an *entire weekend*. A *weekend*! I hadn't done that since I played Pips in Brooklyn twelve years earlier. That was going to be impossible. I'm a comic—that's when we work! Bad enough that every Friday and Saturday night in Rosewood, I was working on myself instead of just plain working like I had for the past seventeen years. Now I had to spend the weekend humor-free—with a sign around my neck heralding it: "No humor. If I make a joke or any attempt at humor, call me on it!" Hmmm, come to think about it, I think Sandra Bernhard had a similar sign hanging around her neck during her last one-woman show.

With humor gone as my last defense, I had no idea what I

was going to do. I thought and I thought, and I finally came up with a plan. I would stop being Robin Williams (code for "needy attention whore") and start being Billy Crystal (self-serious Hollywood type). Switching modes right then and there in the smoking pit, I said, as casually as I could, "Oh, I almost forgot. I should probably text Jim."

Let me explain: Right before I went into Rosewood, I landed a pilot deal for a weekly show on HBO, due in large part to Jim Carrey. See, Jim Carrey is my guardian angel—the guy who discovered me almost a year before and who wanted to develop a TV show based on me. For nearly nine months, we had creative meetings and came up with a dynamite series idea and finally paired up with a brilliant Emmy-winning writer who could breathe life into the show. So, as I sat in Rosewood working on my eating, the contracts for the pilot script were being signed in L.A.

What better way to show the girls—without using humor—that I was somebody? Now, enlightened folks would call this substituting "other esteem" for "self-esteem" since the value I was finding would be not because of who I was on the inside, but because of what I had on the outside, i.e., a connection to one of the most hailed comic actors of our time. But as I sat in the smoking pit, cockblocked from making jokes by Dee the therapist, I needed to feel good somehow and Jim Carrey was the ticket.

"I should probably text Jim." As I expected, one of the girls took the bait.

"Jim who?" she asked anxiously. See, the only time men seemed to be mentioned at Rosewood were when we talked about our non-nurturing, abusive, or emotionally absent fathers, or our non-nurturing, abusive, or emotionally absent boyfriends. So I shattered her hopes of bonding over some horrible man who was beneath us and casually said to her without taking my eyes off my BlackBerry, "Jim Carrey. I'm working on a TV show with him for HBO. Didn't I tell you? I thought I told you that."

Well, *that* got their attention. And I didn't even have to say, "Knock, knock. Who's there?"

"You know Jim Carrey?!?" one of the women who was nearly my age asked in wonderment. "That is sooooo cool. Is he a good guy? He seems like a good guy."

"Have you ever been to his house?" another said, piping up.

"Have you met Jenny McCarthy?"

"What's he really like?"

"Why the fuck did he make *The Majestic*?"

The girls tripped over themselves, lobbing me questions like baseballs at batting practice. And I fielded them all. Yes, he's a good guy. The best. No, I've never been to his house. I was invited once but had to do a gig instead. (You know contracts—you just can't get out of them.) No, I'd never met Jenny but I think she's hilarious. He's really, like, an amazing guy, a genius, a real pro. And best of all, he gets me. And as far as *The Majestic* goes, I have no fuckin' idea.

The girls gazed at me starry eyed. I had gone up a notch in their books.

But you know what they say. Jim giveth and Jim taketh away. And this case was no exception. I sent him a simple text: "Hey, Jim, just wanted to say I miss you, and can't wait to start work on the project"—God, I was cool; I was using industryspeak—"when I'm back in L.A. Love ya and have a great week." I pressed Send and waited. If those girls thought I was on fire before, wait 'til they saw how fast Jim Carrey— *the* Jim Carrey—got back to me. I had no reason to think he wouldn't. In the past, he'd always called back or texted within moments. He'd even left me a glowing congratulatory voice mail when I was nominated for my Grammy.

The seconds ticked by. No response.

"He's probably busy. He could be on vacation with Jenny. I mean, he's really good about taking time out to enjoy life," I vamped as I sensed their interest waning.

As the seconds turned into minutes and the minutes to hours, I was bummed. Jim had been my ace in the hole, the only way I had left to impress the girls, and now unless I could teach them a way to vomit silently without using their fingers, I had nothing.

Two days later, Jim texted me back, thanking me for my message and saying he was excited to work on the project too. Sure! Now he was excited! Where was he two days ago when I was trying to impress a roomful of anorexics? To add insult to injury, I was alone in my room when the text arrived. I shook my head and didn't text back.

❖

By the time I hit my two-week mark at Rosewood, there didn't seem to be much to laugh about. Day after day, I counted the hours 'til I could escape. I looked longingly at my dustier- by-the-minute car as it sat in its sad little space outside my room—mocking me, taunting me. I longed to start it up with the spare key I kept in my bra day and night (that was the only place I could guarantee no one would look—not even the lesbian house moms). I fantasized about cruising down the four-lane Route 60, slowing down only for the speed traps, as I cranked the *Hairspray* or *Grease* soundtrack. (Hey, I'm a fag hag. What'd ya expect? Motörhead?) I'd floor the gas pedal on that Camry and escape for at least an hour. First stop, the 7-Eleven for a decaffeinated Diet Coke. Next stop, a movie theater that played something other than that hideous Indiana Jones Temple of Gloom sequel that was playing at the Wickenburg Theatre what seemed like *every single weekend*. After eating a small box of popcorn—no butter, of course—I would stop by Barnes and Noble and enjoy a decaf latte as I roamed through the stacks of self-help and meditation books. Now, I know that to some of you, this fantasy sounds just as torturous as rehab. At least I wasn't squeezing one out in the bathroom this time. This was progress.

But I was only building a castle in the sky. I would not be allowed to leave Rosewood until I had put in some hard time there, and I was going stir crazy. And as I got more antsy, I got more angry.

I *had* to get out of there! Did these assholes know how much I had sacrificed to come here? I had missed the finale of not only *American Idol* but of my favorite show, *Dancing with the Stars*. And now, the *Sex and the City* movie was coming out—an event that I'd written on my calendar in pink three months earlier!—and I wouldn't be able to see it until *two weeks* after it debuted, when everyone I knew would either have already seen it twice or told me how much it sucked! On top of that, I was feeling so many fucking feelings that I was having discussions—code for "fights"—with patients, therapists, or management on a daily basis.

At that point, the worst was a fight I'd had with the bitch who wouldn't watch any movies that had to do with pregnancy, kids, and birth because of her God-knows-how-many-abortions past. That's right! No *Knocked Up*, no *Juno*, no *Baby Mama*. When I'd pushed to see one of those movies, she manipulated us into watching what she wanted, even though she clearly was in the minority and should have taken herself and her used death-row uterus out of the room. On top of that, I'd apologized to her *when I knew I wasn't wrong*! I should have punched her in the cunt instead, but I think that's against Rosewood rules too. And quite honestly, it sounded like her pussy had been abused enough.

On top of that, we had to cook and do chores. Now, this was weird. Although I am Italian, I have only cooked twice in my life, and as with most single New York City women, my stove has yet to be used for anything other than storage and the occasional suicide attempt. And cleaning! I paid someone to do that—in fact, over the years, my apartment has seen more Mexican women than the East L.A. Ninety-nine Cent Store. But Rosewood was different. Even though I had money, and some of the girls made it clear they could really use it, there was a rule against paying someone to do your chores for you. And the chores were hard—cleaning out the refrigerator, sweeping and mopping the floor, emptying potentially puke-y garbage. If I wanted to do that stuff, I would be house mother at a college fraternity. At least I'd have a chance of getting date raped. I liked that.

I hated this place, I hated everyone in it, and one evening, I'd had it! My day had started out shitty when I lost my serenity rock at the six thirty A.M. twelve-step meeting. Then I got "shamed" by a worker at the gym who said I went over the allowed twenty minutes of exercise on the elliptical (yeah, right—can't you tell by looking at me that *over*exercising is my problem?!?). I was hot, I was irritable, and I was sick of looking at these little bitches running around in their tiny bikinis at pool time when I could barely squeeze my ass into a one-piece from the Delta Burke swimsuit collection. And every time one of these emaciated cunts said they couldn't eat another bite of a plateful of food that wouldn't satisfy a partridge, I wanted to yell, "Eat *this*, bitch!"—which, come to think of it, would be a great name for a reality show based on Rosewood. Note to self: Call my Jew agent.

That night, at our twelve-step meeting for eating disorders, I broke down.

"I don't even deserve to be here," I cried. "I came here voluntarily—I mean, I put *myself* in here, and all you guys are anorexic and bulimic and in danger of dying. I mean, that's heavy. Your health is in serious jeopardy, and I'm just an over-eater. Every time I talk, I feel like I'm taking time out from someone who needs this a lot more than I do." Of course, the same could be said whenever I pop into the Comic Strip for a set. But that's different—I'm trolling for scrotum.

As in all twelve-step meetings, cross-talk—commenting on someone else's share—is discouraged. But the girls of Rose-wood were the only ones at the meeting, so one of them decided to break the rule.

"You are not *just* an overeater. You are not *just* anything," the gorgeous Katy said to me as calmly as could be, as the other girls nodded in agreement. "Your pain is your pain. You are allowed to work on yourself. You are allowed to be here. You *deserve* to be here and help yourself. If we don't work on our issues, we'll be dead in five months. If you don't work on your stuff, you'll be dead in five years. But either way, the result is death."

I replayed Katy's words as I walked across the asphalt parking lot to my private room. It was a hot Arizona night— about ninety degrees—and some of the girls were swimming or lounging at the pool until it would be locked at exactly ten P.M. But instead of envying their bodies and feeling like I wasn't worthy to be with them, I put on my one-piece suit that could have covered three of them and joined them. Then I did a cannonball that drenched every one of those whores. Just kidding. I chatted with them on the tiny deck, and the more we talked, the more we bonded about our problems. By ten o'clock, I realized that my anger had finally disappeared.

Logging on to my computer that night before lights-out, I noticed an e-mail from an acquaintance with the somber subject line "Frank D'Amico died June 1st." I quickly opened the e-mail and read that Frank—Big Frank—had died in L.A. the day before. You remember Big Frank—the four-hundred-pound guy from the beginning of the book, the one who was connected to a fork? Reading about his death, the jokes weren't quite as funny anymore. The only thing I could think about as I finished reading the e-mail were Katy's words from the meeting earlier that night: "You are not *just* an overeater . . . You *deserve* to be here and help yourself . . . you'll be dead in five years. But either way, the result is death."

For Frank, the ex-boyfriend with whom I had the greatest times and still have the fondest memories, his "five years" were up. Frank had died from complications from diabetes, a disease he fought most of his adult life. He would be missed by hundreds of people who loved his quick wit, phenomenal storytelling ability, and good heart. But the point wouldn't be missed by me. This was a sign. I *did* deserve to work on myself, and I would. The next day, I woke up at five A.M. as usual but with a new attitude. I was gonna stop fucking around and beat this thing. And the time to start was now.

❀

It was my last day at Rosewood, and even I had to admit I had come a long way. I had gotten used to a new way of eating— six small meals a day—had begun moderately exercising, and had kicked both caffeine and sugar substitutes. Instead of eating when I had bad feelings, I talked about my feelings, felt them, and paid rapt attention in therapy like it was church. I shared in meetings, I cried, I paid attention to what people were saying at the twelve-step meetings (even though several cute guys were welcome distractions), and I had completed all of my assignments except one. But I have a good excuse— that assignment was impossible.

One day in private session with Dee, she told me that in two days, she wanted me to come up with a two-minute stand-up routine that didn't put myself, the audience, or any subject matter down. Who'd this twat think I was—Carrot Top? I told her this was ridiculous. I wasn't Seinfeld—I didn't talk about cotton balls or missing socks. I was an *insult comic,* but I was a lovable one who didn't harm a soul. So, since my audience didn't get mad at me, why should I write a two-minute bit that went completely against everything I was as a comedian?

"I have my reasons. And notice the feelings that come up when you do it," Dee said. I just shook my head. I wasn't gonna bomb on my last day at Rosewood. If she brought it up Monday, I would say I forgot. But something happened on Monday that made Dee forget about the assignment once and for all.

At nine A.M., I was packed and ready to go. My suitcases bulged with all the cute clothes I had brought and never worn since I had chosen to dress in army fatigues and khakis during my stay there, as if I was a member of the army at war with Ed. My binders and food plans and all my art projects were taken off the cinder-block walls, where they had been fastened with masking tape, and were safely in the trunk of my Toyota. I would transport them to my house at Canyon Ranch in Tucson so I could refer to them if I ever needed a reminder of what I had learned in the joint. Or, more than likely, ignore them until I moved again and threw them away.

Strolling to the main building of what would be my last nine A.M. community meeting, I was at peace. Well, at peace with almost everything. See, during my last two weeks at Rosewood, I had worked hard. But there was one thing I couldn't conquer. A girl named Kim had come into the facility two weeks before, and she was everything I hated in a person. Passive-aggressive, abrasive, abusive, sarcastic—the definition of the word "cunt." Think Rosie O'Donnell with better punch lines. As I entered the room, I saw her sitting on the corner of one of the couches and I sat as far away as I could, on a straight-backed chair near the arts and crafts table.

Now, Rosewood uses something called "The Feedback Loop." This is a tool that was developed by therapist Pia Mellody at the Meadows, another rehab in Wickenburg. The Feedback Loop aids in communicating feelings. Instead of saying something like "You took the last cookie, you fucking asshole. What do you think, you're more important than me? I hate you when you do that. You should die of cancer," Pia says people should communicate their feelings in the following manner: "When you took the last cookie without asking me if I wanted it, what I made up about that was that I was not as important as you, and about that I felt sadness, anger, and frustration."

Once someone receives such a statement, he or she should take it in, not take it personally, and decide what to say or do in a mature way.

Well, needless to say, this was a whole new way of communicating for me and most of the girls there. But thanks to community meeting each and every day at nine in the morning, we had the opportunity to practice The Feedback Loop on people in the Rosewood community. Most of the time, the girls—including myself—punked out and said stuff that wasn't directed at any one particular member of the group. Stuff like "When people leave their unwashed dishes in the sink, what I make up about that is that my need for order and cleanliness in the kitchen is not a priority, and about that I feel pain, shame, and sadness."

But today was going to be different. I had heard through one of the more gossipy girls there that Kim was mad at me because I hadn't let her sit with me at dinner two nights before when we were on our Saturday-night outing to a local Mexican restaurant. (Yes, this is the kind of thing that seems important when you're cut off from reality for twenty-eight days.) My feeling was that I didn't like her, and I didn't have to sit with her on the one night I was allowed to escape from Rosewood.

Now, guaranteed, I could have been nicer about it. As three of the women who were around my age and I ate our pre-meal chips and salsa, a dozen or so of the younger women sat at a table in an adjacent room. As she entered the restaurant, Kim spotted us and made a beeline right for the table.

"You can eat in there," I said dismissively as I put my hand in the air and pointed to where the other girls were sitting, adding a talk-to-the-hand flip as an accent. I resumed my meal at the cunt-free table.

I know, I know. I told you I could have been nicer.

In the two days since the restaurant occurrence, ever since I'd heard Kim was angry with me, my anger had begun to simmer. But now, as I sat in the community room, my insides were bubbling, and I became more and more resolved to Feedback Loop the bitch. She was gonna get it with both barrels from me. And the beauty of The Feedback Loop was, she wasn't allowed to interrupt.

As the girls went around the room and did their usual safe, lame statements—"When the staff walked into my room unannounced, what I made up about that was my privacy is not respected, and about that I feel blah, blah, blah"—I formulated my exact wording for maximum impact.

Finally, it was my turn, and my blood was boiling and my heart was racing. I felt like a teakettle about to whistle—*loudly*.

I looked directly at Kim—or, more precisely, at a spot on the wall above her head. (I've never been particularly good at eye contact.)

I spoke in an even tone with a terse expression on my face.

"When I am gossiped about because I express an interest in eating dinner with only the people I choose"—I shot the three older women a look—"what I make up about that is that my decisions are not my own nor are they respected, and about that I feel anger."

As I expected, Kim's hand shot up.

She opened her clammy little mouth to speak: "When I overhear that I am called a cunt . . ."

How dare she bring up the fact that I called her a cunt! Clearly, I was being wronged here. "Well, if you're *called a cunt*," I bellowed with all the repressed anger—and volume—of the last twenty-eight days, "it's because *you are a cunt!*"

A collective gasp went up in the room. Nobody interrupted The Feedback Loop. It was sacred. Pia Mellody hadn't designed it that way. Oh, no!!! What would Pia think?!?

"Oh, yeah?" Kim shot back, her piglike little eyes blinking away. "Well, I'm happy you're leaving."

And in the blink of an eye, I turned from Lisa Lampanelli: Self-Helper to Lisa Lampanelli: Fiercest Insult Comedian on the Planet.

"Oh, really, well, you're the only one who's glad I'm leaving. Seriously, who's glad I'm leaving?" I spit out the words with outstretched hands as I looked around the room from girl to girl, just as I'd done countless times onstage when dealing with a heckler. It was the rehab version of the comedian's "Who came to hear this asshole? And who came to hear *me?*"

The girls shook their heads. Most of them clearly liked me,

and they murmured variations of "Not me. I like you. You should stay."

Clearly the crowd was on my side and I decided to roll with it. "See, you fucking cunt," I shrieked at Kim. "Nobody wants me to leave. But trust me, they want *you* to leave, you cocksucking bitch!" Suddenly, this wasn't rehab anymore. It was a sorority.

With that, the nurse burst into the room to see what all the yelling was about. Yelling was allowed in therapy—like when we were screaming at empty chairs that represented our parents or people who had cornholed us as kids—but yelling was *never* allowed in community meetings.

As the nurse flew in to try to restore order, I screamed, tears streaming down my face, "I've had it with this shit!!" and with that, I stormed out the door, slamming it *hard,* another no-no in rehab.

After about an hour with all three therapists, where there was much crying, reading from the Big Book of Alcoholics Anonymous, and Feedback Looping—God, I couldn't get away from that shit—I had calmed down. I resolved to "make amends" to Kim—an action that was one of the biggies in twelve-step programs—for interrupting her and for calling her names. I, however, was not going to apologize for my feelings. Those were valid. I went downstairs and joined the group.

As I entered the therapy session already in progress, I noticed Kim's seat on the couch was vacant. "Good," I thought. "I can put off that amends shit until after lunch." But moments later, Kim entered the room with a stumble. She flopped down in her seat and within ten minutes, her head slumped onto the arm of the couch with a thud.

"Kim," the therapist said. "Kim. Where were you?"

She raised her head slightly and with slurred words said, "I was in my room. I took two sleeping pills and three anxiety pills." And with that, her head thudded back onto the arm of the sofa.

Later that day, Kim was taken away to Rosewood's main building—the intense inpatient hospitalization place—where she, from what we heard, caused such a ruckus that she was removed and sent to a psychiatric hospital. This was a first for me. Usually, when I call someone a cunt, they just ask the theater for their money back.

For a moment, I felt slightly guilty, like I had caused her to take those pills. But I remembered what the therapists had told us day after day: "You are not responsible for anyone else's feelings or actions. You are only responsible for your own."

Remembering that, I realized that I had had nothing to do with Kim's apparent suicide attempt. She did what she did because of her own demons.

But part of me took a little pride in knowing that once again, I was killing—almost literally—in rehab.

part four

It's Only Upward
from Here!

The Future of

Lisa Lampanelli

ell, it's been exactly six months since I left Rosewood and I've been relatively great—well, as great as a codependent food-addicted comedian can be.

Since getting out of the joint, I have a new shrink—a New York Jew who's tough but fair and who keeps pushing me to be more vulnerable with people and show them my real self. I guess writing this book is a start. Maybe by the time it comes out, I will have had the balls to call my brother and tell him "I love you" for no reason, but for now, I have to be content with writing it in an e-mail. And my sister? My Jew shrink wants me to call her and tell her how much I admire her—*out of the blue*! I told him if I start doing those things, they'll think I'm dying of cancer or something. So, for now, their mentions in the acknowledgments of this book will have to do.

As far as my eating goes, I haven't emotionally eaten in the six months since I left Rosewood, but I have to admit, I do nigger-rig my food plan every now and then (I can eat a muffin the size of a baby's head instead of two kiwis, can't I? They both only count as two starches, right?). Well, like they say in the twelve-step meetings, it's progress, not perfection, and I have made progress since the days of stuffing my anger and loneliness with a box of Hostess Cupcakes.

When it comes to my weight, at the time of this writing, I have lost a couple of pounds but gone are the days when it comes off easily. At forty-eight, it creeps off slowly, but honestly, I'm just relieved to be on the way down instead of on the way up. Hopefully, by the time you're reading this, I will have either lost the fifteen pounds I had yearned to lose when I entered Rosewood, or I will have accepted that this is my weight and that it's good enough for me. (Believe it or not, Jew shrink thinks it's possible for me to look in the mirror and like what I see.) And the last time I was on Howard's show, he, like Bubba, called me skinny too. Sometimes when people really like you, they also like what they see.

As far as the friends and enemies I made in my various rehabs, there are some I keep in touch with and some I don't. Obviously, crazy Kim and I aren't exactly bosom buddies—in fact, when I played her home state recently, I gave a photo of her to my security guard so he could keep a watch out for her in case she tried to kill me. Needless to say, she didn't. Although I've lost touch with most of the people from my 2007 codependency rehab, I keep in very close contact with my three friends from the first food addiction group—Kyle, Karen, and Charlotte—and I count them among the few people I can call at four in the morning in case I need to talk. On the other hand, I have little contact with the girls of Rosewood. This is probably due to the intense feelings that come up when I think of talking to them. But hopefully, by the time this book is published, we will all be back in touch and maybe even have a reunion where they actually keep their food down. But if any of you Rosewood bitches are reading this, know that I love you all and think of you daily, and chuckle remembering our times around that table doing the Rosewood cheer.

When it comes to my twelve-step meetings, I don't attend them as often as I should. At last count, it's been about three weeks since I've gone to one. That being said, it's a real comfort knowing that whenever I decide to get off my ass and go to a meeting, there are eight thousand to choose from in New York City. There are meetings for overeaters (where you can't name specific foods in case it would trigger someone. In fact, in one meeting, a woman referred to a birthday cake as a "round thing with candles." I nearly became a puker on the spot). There are meetings for codependents, and there are meetings for every other addiction I may or may not take up by the time you're reading this. So it's nice to know that free help is just a few blocks away.

As far as men go, I still receive the occasional text from Tommy but, of course, have not responded. Tommy, if you're reading this, it's nothing personal. I have no anger toward you, and I wish you nothing but the best. And fuck you for not buying this book but borrowing it from somebody else. Regarding other men, I have good news to report. After taking enough time off to get to know the real me and get comfortable with being alone, I began dating again. After a few false starts, the unimaginable happened: I fell in love with a cuddly bear of a man who loves me back. Now I finally see what love without codependency feels like. And what it feels like can be summed up in one word: *magic!*

Oh, uh, and for all of you who ask, "Lisa Lampanelli, is he black?" Guess you'll have to read the sequel to this book to find out.

Professionally, things couldn't be better. My one-hour special *Long Live the Queen* debuted on HBO in January '09, and I recently sold out the world-famous Radio City Music Hall in New York City. And that sitcom produced by Jim Carrey? Well, we just handed in the script to HBO, so by the time you read this, I'm either part of a wildly successful weekly TV show on the best channel on TV, or I'm just another comic who had a pilot that never aired. Either way, I'll survive. Hell, I'll just blame it on the writing.

As far as how I see my future, who the fuck knows? I do have a few fantasies. Like, I could suddenly wake up maternal at fifty and decide to adopt two children like Diane Keaton did, but by then, I'll probably only have a spoiled dog and a droopy plant. I also dream that someday I will finish one of the six dozen self-help books that line my shelves and windowsills. Lastly, I would like to write a miniseries about my rich history with men of the African-American race—kind of like *Roots* but not as funny.

I guess all I do know is that I'm the happiest I've ever been in my life since those carefree days of high school. And for now, that's good enough for me.

You know, my father says he always reads the first line and the last line of a story to see if he's going to like it. So, since that's what he'll probably do with this book and since the first line of my story was the surely disappointing-to-him "Once you go black . . . ," I'd like to leave him with a good final line instead:

I would like to say that in the future, I hope to be the little girl my dad always wanted—sweet, gentle, and shy. I would also like a team shower with the Miami Dolphins, but that ain't gonna happen either. So I guess my old man will just have to settle for an obnoxious, rough, loudmouthed bitch who makes enough money to get him a private room at the nursing home. In advance, Dad, you're welcome!

part five

Lisa's Rules
to Live By

As most of my fans know by now, Lisa Lampanelli has an opinion on everything—even things I know absolutely nothing about. So, as a parting gift to you, dear reader, I have included some random thoughts and musings on everything from addiction to xenophobia for your perusal, entertainment, and perhaps most important, your edification.

Part One: What I'm Known For . . .

. . . .

"Once You Go Black . . ."

People always ask me if the saying "Once you go black, you never go back" is true. To that, I answer—yes! It's true because once you go black, you never have to go to another family reunion. You never have to be in another person's wedding either, because they don't want a black smudge on their wedding photo.

Don't get me wrong—you could go back to dating white guys, but it'd be hard to return to them with their jobs and their one-woman-at-a-time policy. But come to think of it, why would you want to go back to whitey? Sure, with black guys, you may never get your front yard landscaped, but you'll get your backyard expertly plowed. When you date the blacks you can weigh two hundred and still be considered skinny. Going out to eat is a lot easier when you don't have to tip, and there are some shows on the WB that you simply don't want to miss.

Cooking for a black man is easy too. Just fry the crap out of everything! He'll love it—I guarantee it will taste better than anything he got in jail. Sure, you might have to put up with being called a bitch and a ho, but the sex is worth it.

In short, the saying *is* absolutely true. After the brothas, where's a bitch to go? I make enough money on my own that I don't need a white guy and his fancy salary. And when you take away income potential from the white guy, what are you left with? A small dick and a polo shirt! Italians? They all like to pretend they're in the mob. The last Italian I dated never said he came, he would just say his dick sleeps with the fishes. Latinos? I have a hard enough time understanding what the blacks are trying to say. Besides, I like my relationships to last longer than migration season. Asians? Not those cheap bastards. The last one I dated wouldn't even give me a discount on my dry cleaning after he dripped duck sauce on my back.

At least I assumed it was duck sauce. Jews? No way. They require 15 percent down just to eat your pussy.

No—it's the black man for me. Now, I'm outta here. I gotta go post some bail.

Black Women Hating on Brothers Who Date White Women

Black women hate black men who date white women for a very important reason: Who else is going to date a black woman? A white man may get his jungle love on at a strip club, but he's not bringing Shanequa home to Mom and Dad. He may want to father a professional athlete but he figures it's easier to teach his kid tennis than deal with a crazy nappy-headed ho who's bigger than him and not afraid of jail. An Asian's not going to date a black woman. His little dick will get lost in a vag that was built to take on elephant cock. Latinos? No way! They hate blacks more than whites because they think blacks gave minorities a bad name, and they have to share the same social services. Even if a Latino man was attracted to a black woman, he would never get past Maria. All Latinas are named Maria, and they're very territorial and good with a knife.

Don't get me wrong—I don't think it's right for black women to hate all black men who date white women. Sure, I can see that when we're talking professional athletes or the few other ones who have a job. But when black women get angry when you date your run-of-the-mill, prepaid-cell-phone, living-with-his-mama black guy, that's plain ridiculous.

I myself am not above prejudice when it comes to some types of interracial couples. For example, I hate when a good-looking, skinny white girl dates a black man, because she can

get a good white one. I don't know which is worse about seeing a brother roll into the club with a pretty white girl—the
look of pride on his face, like he just won an ESPY, or the condescending look on her face, like she is somehow above petty
things in life like race, class, and gender roles when it comes to
paying for drinks. Skinny bitches, hear my plea! Leave the hot
black men for the chubby bitches who need them.

Black Men Who Live with Their Moms or Grandmoms

People get down on black men who live with their moms,
but that is not fair. Black men need to live with their moms
because who can pay rent with the price of basketball shoes
going up every day? Besides, when the whole family is under one roof, you don't have to look any farther than the living room couch to find a capable accomplice. Black men like
to live with their mothers and grandmothers because, quite
frankly, no one can be expected to eat at McDonald's at *every*
meal *every* day.

For a black man, the advantages of living with his mom or
grandmom are virtually endless. First of all, black men like to
have someone they can trust with the story when the po-po
comes. Their baby mamas wouldn't think twice about sending
them to jail. But not Mama—she needs help with the bills.
Plus, pit bulls like Mom's backyard more than the deck off a
one-bedroom apartment. And last but not least, Mom always
has a menthol you can bum on the way out the door.

I think it's funny, however, when a black man lives with his
mom or grandmom and then tries to act like he's doing her
a favor. "My mom needs me to help take care of her." Really,
Tyrone? Your mom is still in her thirties and gives you an

allowance. The only thing you help her with is her exercise when she bends over to pick up your soiled undies. Your mom hasn't wanted you around since you turned eighteen and WIC stopped counting you as a dependent. And by the way, if you can't afford rent for your own apartment, you are no longer allowed to wear large gold dollar-sign medallions.

I dated a black man who lived with his grandmom. He always said, "Well, Grams needs a man around." Yeah, Grams needs a man who is courteous and helps her with her errands, not some selfish prick who sleeps all day and then steals her social security money so he can feel like a big shot at the club drinking Grand Marnier. And by the way, brothas, if you're going to bring a girl back to Grandma's, have the decency to not do your screaming and ass slapping in the very next room. Hearing aids can only be turned down so low.

Black Men's Credit, Cell Phones, Tipping, and Other Nonexistent Entities

It is unfair to say that black men do not have credit. Black men do have credit—it's just not at the bank. It's with the local bookie, drug dealer, and/or pimp. That's right, bitches—Leroy is diversified. To get credit at a savings establishment, you need to keep your money in a bank. The black man keeps his money in his sock, a trait he learned from his mama, who kept hers in her bra. Black men don't invest in stocks and bonds— they invest in rims, basketball shoes, and throwback jerseys. I call them "throw-up jerseys" because nothing is more nauseating than a grown man wearing a Dr. J jersey with an undershirt on underneath so you can't see his man titties.

One thing black men do have are cell phones. They usually have two—their regular one and one their baby's mama doesn't know about. But a black man's cell phone is not just a cell phone—it's a boom box, movie theater, and porn store rolled into one. A black man's cell phone is the most sophisticated thing he owns besides his PlayStation 3. And black men know how to work those phones. He may not know how to open a Word document but he can download a Nelly ringtone and send it with a text in picture mail to his brother from another mother.

FYI: Black people are the reason certain places automatically include gratuity. I didn't know this until I started noticing that at comedy clubs, it was always the black people pissed off about included gratuities. "I always tip." Then why are you so pissed? Now you don't even need to do the math. "What if they don't deserve a tip?" Hey, you ran them back to the kitchen twenty times to get hot sauce for your potato skins and to have the bartender put more booze in your drink. Trust me, they deserve a tip.

Does Size Matter? Is the Myth True?

Does size matter? Of course it does. Like the old saying goes: You need the right-size key to open the lock. It doesn't have to be one of those keys the mayor gives you to the city, but it shouldn't be a key for your luggage lock either. Women don't want anything too huge. You don't want to deep-throat someone and crack a rib. Sometimes a cock is too big and gets in the way. Like the time I sat on Santa's lap and he was halfway up my chimney.

That being said, men care more about dick size than women do. Guys with big dicks are confident—that's why they get more pussy. If they had more confidence, guys with small dicks could get just as much pussy—they just wouldn't get as many repeat customers. You can tell a guy has a small dick by looking in his eyes. It's a secret he wants to tell you but can't.

To tell you the truth, I'm more concerned about the size of a guy's balls. One time I was sixty-nining a guy and came home with two black eyes.

Some people swear by the old adage "It's not the size of the boat, it's the motion of the ocean." That may be true, but it's been my experience that the ocean moves about the same no matter what boat you're in, so it might as well be a luxury liner. The women didn't jump into the little boats until *after* the *Titanic* sank. I like a penis so big I don't know whether to grab it or feed it a peanut. A little penis is like an egg roll— five minutes later, you're hungry again. But a big penis is like a buffet—when it's over, you sit there with your pants undone, moaning, "Why did I eat all that?"

There are, however, some advantages to a little penis. For example, if you're not in the mood, you can still do it and barely notice. Also, if you get a divorce, you're not ruined for anyone else.

The biggest problem with a man with a small penis is all the extra expense—the Hummer truck, the weight-lifting equipment, the huge house. No offense, but why don't we just stuff your pants with a sock and drop that second mortgage?

Black Names

Black people have the most ridiculous names. They make it so you have to call them a racial slur because you can't pro- nounce their real name. Now, I don't mean their gang names or the names they get when they join a bastard religion, I mean the names their mamas give them. I know they can't be named after their fathers because they don't know who they are, but black people are named like the Scrabble game fell on the floor. Blacks name their kids after cars they have to steal to get their hands on, like Porsche and Mercedes. Some black names sound like STDs—Syphalinda readily comes to mind. Some blacks go French and add a "Le-" to regular names like Roy to get "Leroy." Girl names always seem to have an "-isha" or an "-anda" at the end. Those must be Swahili for "ho." Shaniqua, Tawanda, Propecia. I can't tell if these are people's names or something men rub into their scalp. I actually tried to spell-check "Shaniqua." The computer suggested that I "just call that bitch Sharon."

Some black people say these are family names. I beg to disagree. All the old black women I know are named Shirley or Jemima. And don't act like you are trying to get back to your African roots either. In Uganda, if you name a girl Lakeisha, the tribe takes you out of the village and has you stoned.

As Americans, however, it is our right to name our child anything, even if it is something ridiculous. But if you choose to do so, you don't have the right to complain when you can't find a "Laquetta" key chain at Cedar Point. And it's not your daughter's first-grade teacher's fault when she keeps mispronouncing the name "Tangenika."

Professional Athletes

All boys who aren't gay grow up wanting to be professional athletes. However, what they don't realize is this means they'll be addicted to painkillers, crippled by forty, and dead by sixty. If the steroids don't rot their brains, the constant adulation does. A pro athlete is more selfish than a four-year-old only child. Pro athletes play games for a living and then bitch when they don't think they're getting enough money. Who would think dunking a basketball is worth more than saving someone from a burning building? But pro athletes need all that money to pay all of their child support. Getting knocked up by a pro athlete is the ghetto version of winning the lottery.

Pro athletes spend most of their time in strip clubs, but when they do the occasional good deed for charity, it's reported like a moon landing. All they have to do is go to a hospital and hand out free shit and they're treated like Jesus, while the nurses who are there 24/7 get rocks thrown at them if they go on strike for better health benefits.

Professional athletes prove that money doesn't solve all your problems. It just pays for the lawyers so you don't have to suffer the consequences. These athletes always travel in a posse from their old neighborhood, not because they enjoy their company, but because they need someone to take the rap if the cops find marijuana in their car. And, trust me, they always have marijuana. They keep it right under the gun that's registered in their cousin's name. You would think that if you got paid millions of dollars to play a game, you might want to avoid places where you could get shot. You're rich, a-hole! Stay out of the titty bars! Learn from Donald Trump. Buy yourself a beauty pageant and then tell the runner-up if she blows you you'll disqualify the winner.

*Part Two: How the Hell I Turned Out This Way . . .
Macy's and Hamburger's*

. . . .

Pregnant Women in the Workplace

Pregnant women are appearing in more workplaces because the economy sucks so bad a woman needs to work until the kid is crawling down her leg. And, boy, do these women love being pregnant at work! Every pregnant broad is treated like a queen and she has an excuse for everything. It's like she's having her time of the month for three-quarters of a year. She can cry anytime she wants to and she's suddenly entitled to the biggest piece of cake at the office parties. And of course, the cow *loves* all the attention. She is the star at every meeting, she gets to put her feet up, and if she falls asleep, no one gets mad. Plus she gets to burp like a trucker and fart like a middle-schooler, and everyone turns a blind eye because she can sue if anyone says a damn thing.

I don't like when women work up until the point they have the baby. What is this, Communist China? Asian women pick rice, have a baby, put it in a backpack, and keep going. No, people! This is America, and trust me, our people aren't working that hard to begin with. What's the worst thing that could happen if you send a pregnant woman home a month early— fewer forwarded joke e-mails that involve kittens? Who gives a shit? Clearly, a woman needs to work for the first several months after she gets pregnant, for no other reason than her male coworkers enjoy watching her tits get bigger. After that, she should just stay home.

Seriously, who wants a woman in her ninth month waddling

around the office, carrying a towel in case her water breaks? Plus, the bitch is always leaving meetings early because she has to pee. These women can't be given any long-term projects, because you never know when they're going to be gone. Quite honestly, working with a woman who's nine months pregnant is like working with a black guy. She's moody, defensive, and you never know when she's gonna stop showing up.

Epidurals vs. Natural Childbirth

Natural childbirth sounds great on paper but when you're trying to pull a person out of your hole, it's good to have some drugs. So take my advice, pregnant beeyotches—sign up for them early. Don't let some hippie cunt trick you into thinking all you need are positive vibes. If you wait until your legs are in the air, it will be too damned late.

Some women are against epidurals because they don't want drugs in the child's system. Hey, Mom of the Year, did you forget about the eight ball you did the night little Jessica was conceived? And besides, wouldn't you rather your baby came into the world with a little drug hangover and without bleeding eardrums from you screaming "*Fuck!!!!*" at the top of your lungs for eight hours straight?

Feminists and people without health care try to go au naturel and don't even go to the hospital. They have a midwife—also known as a "maid with special training"—and attempt to give birth at home. These people always end up at the hospital anyway when the baby is coming out sideways and the stoned midwife is on the phone with her boyfriend back in Holland. Birthing at home? No, thanks. I'll have mine in a public place under the influence of drugs—just like the conception.

Natural childbirth people say delivery without drugs is better for the baby. So what? So is breastfeeding them for two years and actually knowing who their dad is, but that doesn't mean I'm doing it. And let's be honest, when this kid is a teenager who's wrecking my cars and sleeping with people in my bed, I'm going to be glad I didn't provide the little extras like natural childbirth or spending time with them.

Seriously, I can't imagine having a natural childbirth when you consider the fact that epidurals are available. Let me see if I have this right: I can have hours of excruciating pain as I pass a human skull through an orifice that previously had a three-finger limit, or I can have a shot and basically not feel a thing? Hmmm. If I was willing to freely accept that much pain, I wouldn't have spent my whole life fighting off anal. I think I'll take the shot. Hell, I needed one this morning and all I was doing was pinching a loaf. Note to self: Eat more fiber.

Husbands and Other Useless Entities in the Delivery Room

Recently, it has become popular to turn the delivery room into a cocktail party with guests enjoying snacks and breezy conversation while Mom is getting tortured. They think it's going to be fun to watch until they spend some time there. Every type of bodily function is on display and coming at you in 3-D. It's like a Gallagher concert, except it's entertaining. And the blood! Oh, the blood. The vagina looks like it owed the Gambinos money and didn't pay up.

Men especially should be banned from the delivery room. They're always in the way and, to quote Jack, "can't handle the truth." The truth is that the thing they liked best about their woman has just been 9/11'ed. Waiting outside and handing out cigars is much better for men than seeing their happiest place on earth destroyed under bright lights. You know what they say—if you love eating at a restaurant, you should never go in the kitchen and see how the food is made.

Why is the father expected to be in the delivery room these days anyway? Clearly, they're no help. And we give them patronizing titles like "coach." "Okay, I want you to spread your legs and have your twat run the picket fence. And if that doesn't work, put your finger up your ass and run the Statue of Liberty." Wow! Thanks, Bear Bryant.

Let's face it—the man is in the delivery room for one reason and one reason only: Women want him to see how horrible it is. Why? For a lot of reasons. First and foremost, we're not going to feel like having sex for several months, and if he sees your twat the size of a trash can lid, he's not going to want to either.

Second, this is the one chance we have of telling him what a douchebag he is without having to listen to him attack us back. It's perfect—the woman can say horrible things, and because she's having a baby, he has to take it and apologize. I honestly believe this is why some women have ten kids.

Passing Down the Family Name

People feel the need to pass on their entire name to their offspring, as if the last name ain't bad enough. Why give the kid both names? It's a well-known fact that nobody likes sequels.

Passing down the family name from generation to generation makes sense if you were a president or a pillar of society.

However, if your job includes a shovel or clip-on tie, it's time to give your kid a break. Think about it: Would you enjoy being called "Little Pete" or "Junior" your entire life? Of course not. And besides, what if your kid turns out to be a fuckup? That's *your* name. Do you think former president George Bush likes to be confused with recent president George Bush? Hell, no! It's gotten so bad, former president Bush has changed his name to Jimmy Carter to avoid the stigma.

The worst is when a man wants a boy so badly he gives his daughter his name with a girl ending. Like Joelene—the pathetic female equivalent of Joel. Men with the "III"s and the "IV"s after their name just sound like fags but they have enough money to buy and sell you, so you have to pretend it's cool.

And what if your name is an old-school weirdo name? Now you have to get beat up every day at school because your great-grandpa's name was Irving.

There's another name phenomenon that is often seen in the South. Dale Earnhardt Jr. Hank Williams Jr. It turns out "junior" is a Latin word that means "half the talent of my old man."

Family Trees/Genealogy

Family trees only matter if you're betting on a horse or want to be a made member of the mob. Everyone's family tree starts with a monkey and ends in disappointment. Unless you're owed a chunk of cash, how does knowing who your ancestors are change your life? Your ancestors' story and five dollars will get you a cup of coffee at Starbucks.

People who brag about their family tree are foolish. If you

shake anybody's family tree hard enough, rotten fruit will fall out. Family trees are important to crazy cults like Mormons and Nazis because they want to make sure all of their followers are too weak to have their own thoughts. That's because it's the mixing of genes that makes them stronger. Everybody knows that mutts from the pound are ten times healthier than purebred yellow Labs whose bones break when they run.

I can sort of see why adopted people would want to dig up their family trees, in order to find out what diseases they're genetically predisposed to. For example, I find it a huge advantage that I know my family background, so I can blame my sluttiness, bitchiness, and bad temper on genetics rather than on personal decisions I've made.

I also understand why black people want to find out about their roots. If they dig back far enough, maybe they'll find out they're related to Thomas Jefferson. And we all know there's no better way to piss off whitey!

People Who Are Way Too Proud to Be from "the Old Country"

I'm sick of people coming to America and telling us how great their old country was. I'm not some kind of "America—love it or leave it" asshole, but if you came to America, stop bitching about it. If your home country was so great, you wouldn't have left. The prouder people are of where they're from, the bigger a shithole it usually is—like the Bronx.

I hate these former foreigners who get annoyed when we don't know where their country is on a map. Oh, c'mon! Most Americans can't find Canada on a map. In short, if we've never been at war with you, we don't know where your country is.

These people are always complaining about the things they can't get here that were plentiful over there—like malaria and rape. They don't understand American customs like voting and freedom. They say our women dress like whores but that's because our women don't have to cover up because there's no money for heating oil. And they don't want their kids corrupted with crazy ideas, like money and fun.

People are too proud to be from the old country. It doesn't make any sense. Who cares if your great-great-grandfather was from Ireland? Be proud he moved to a place that can grow potatoes every year. And if you're Italian, pull the olive oil out of your ass and quit bragging about Sicily. The only reason you're even here is because one of your grandmas shamed the family by banging a Greek.

Black people are always pining about Africa, except the ones who have enough money to visit Africa. The minute they go there, they burn their dashikis and start wearing flag pins. And Cubans shouldn't act all high and mighty. If your country was worth a shit, you wouldn't have drifted over here in an apple crate. And I don't want to hear it from the Mexicans either. If your country was as great as you say it is, you wouldn't have snuck over here to clean our toilets.

I like the Asians. They learn the language and useful skills like how to give a massage with release. That's all you can really ask for from an immigrant. The only time Asians get mad is when you call them the wrong kind of Asian: "Me not Japanese. Me Korean." What's the difference? You don't drink sake while you eat your dog? You'll still do my nails, right?

The ones that piss me off the most are the Canadians. They have every advantage. They look like us, they talk like us, and then when we bomb a country or refuse to give medical treatment to homeless people, they act all offended. But once they come here, they never leave! They just bitch and bitch and keep taking our money. Congratulations, Canucks! You have officially assimilated.

Sibling Rivalry

Sibling rivalry is the oldest psychological affliction known to man. It's the reason Cain killed Abel. Their mom, Eve, liked Abel more.

Sibling rivalry can be a good thing among well-adjusted kids from functional families. You see examples of this on television when the sports announcer says, "Steve and his brother Mike are both in the majors, but we hear his younger brother Joe is the best one of them all." Most of the time, though, sibling rivalry is used by less-than-perfect parents to get the best out of one of the kids and the worst out of the rest. People who never lived up to an older sibling have paid for more drinks at psychiatrists' conventions than American Express.

Sibling rivalry comes from the core ego in all people. We naturally want to be the best at everything, and to start, we need to be the best in our own house. To add to the pressure, being in most families is like being in the Olympics. People only remember who won the gold.

That said, the entertainment world owes its existence to sibling rivalry. If comedy clubs only booked comics who got attention when they were kids, their stages would be empty, and if lap dances were only given by people who were unconditionally loved by their parents, the crisis facing the world would be a stripper shortage, not an oil shortage.

I think sibling rivalry has a lot to do with birth order, because you rarely see twins dislike each other. As a matter of fact, most of the twins I've seen have always been naked in *Playboy*, rubbing each other's asses. Even the thought of hugging my older sister naked horrifies me. Of course, she's kind of heavy, so maybe I'm just shallow.

Brothers are especially weird. The only person you'll kick the shit out of faster than your brother is anyone who fucks with your brother. Brothers treat each other like Inflate-a-Mates. They'll do horrible twisted shit to one, but the thought of anyone else touching him makes them sick to their stomachs.

Of course, all families have the good one and the bad one. Every kid's goal should be to be the good one but to marry the bad one. That way, your spouse's parents won't give a shit if you come for Thanksgiving or not. It makes the holidays—and life—a lot less complicated.

Sharing a Bathroom

Sharing a bathroom is an activity that brings families closer together and further apart at the same time. You're closer together because you know exactly what your father's shit smells like after pizza, and you're further apart because you accidentally flushed the toilet while your sister was in the shower, giving her third-degree burns.

Sharing a bathroom is like being in the military. It requires skills, extensive planning, and the will to overcome hell. You must be a multitasker with the ability to brush your teeth and hold your nose at the same time. And it takes Pentagon planning to get everyone showered and out the door by seven thirty A.M.

The only other place you'll find the hell endured in sharing a bathroom is war. If you've ever had to hold back a Stanley Steamer because of a locked door after having a stomachache all day, you know what I mean. The only thing grosser than the unknown hair on the soap in the tub is standing in the shower in a foot of lukewarm water, since the drain is always half-clogged, watching your future nieces and nephews come floating by.

Even worse than sharing a bathroom as a kid is sharing a bathroom as an adult. There's something self-defeating about cleaning yourself in the shower while your better or worse half takes a shit in the same room. Even a cat won't lick itself in a litter box. And as every parent knows, the frustration doubles when you share a bathroom with a boy who's just hit puberty. Great! I have to wait forty-five minutes to wax my mustache just because Jessica Alba is on the cover of *Cosmo*. Now not only am I going to be late for work, I'm gonna have to throw away our hand towels.

Italian Families vs. Normal Families

Italian families are different from normal families. And by "normal," I mean WASP families. There are many reasons for these differences. The first is volume. Italians whispering is screaming to a WASP.

When normal families scream and degrade each other, they go to therapy. In Italian families, the screaming and degrading *is* the therapy. Normal dads will whisper something like "It's quiet time" or "Use your inside voice." Italian dads will yell, "Shut your mouth, you stupid fuck." And that's at his baby's baptism.

Italians also need to hug, kiss, and basically molest each other constantly. If you need personal space, don't hang out with Italians. Italians are a very loving people, and if you don't believe that, you'll get smacked. In fact, a smack and a kiss are synonymous in most Italian families.

Italian moms are the worst. A normal mom puts a bumper sticker on her car with a soccer ball with her son's number in it. An Italian mom puts a hit out on the coach if her son doesn't get to start.

The cocktail cart is the center of the universe in most WASP families, but for Italians, the center of the universe is the dinner table. The dinner table is where everybody eats, plays cards, and stews vendettas.

WASPs make fun of their wives' cooking; an Italian protects his wife's cooking honor like it's his daughter's virginity. The family's sauce, or "gravy," recipe is passed down with pride like the WASPs do with those stupid crests.

Sadly, though, Italian women are not treated as equal to their men. WASP women have come a long way, baby, but Italian men don't want their women going anywhere. Italian women are supposed to be beautiful, great cooks, and, above all else, quiet. If an Italian woman wants to make a big stink and take on the family, she needs to run away first like Madonna or she's gonna get smacked or kissed.

It's a stereotype, but a true one nonetheless, that Italian women are just as hairy as Italian men. WASPs may get waxed and lasered, but for Italian women, it's like fighting the ocean's tide: You'll never get ahead.

That's why Italian girls get married young. When they're twenty, they're big-titted beauties with long dark hair. Thirty years later, those big tits are hip-huggers, the long dark hair is a mustache, and they refer to their husband as "that lazy prick." That might explain why Italian men are so angry.

You don't believe me? Prepare to get smacked.

Sears Portrait Studio

Taking a trip to the Sears Portrait Studio is equal in stress to going to the cemetery to bury the family pet—only with Sears, you get to bring home reminders that last generations.

First of all, it is impossible for anyone being photographed at a Sears Portrait Studio to look his best. That's because the Sears photographer is only a Sears photographer because it pays more than being a Sears cashier. Simply put, he has the artistic eye of Helen Keller.

I actually feel sorry for those kids who work at the Sears Portrait Studio. They spend all day dealing with crying and whining and people shitting their pants—and that's just the mothers who are unhappy with how the photos look. If I ever met one of these entitled soccer twats, I'd say, "Hey, lady, don't bitch at the nineteen-year-old photographer because your baby looks ugly. You should have married better."

Add to that, no one getting photographed at the Sears Portrait Studio can really bring it. The little kids can't smile because they've just been hit for not listening. The teenagers can't smile because their braces hurt or the zits on their foreheads are tugging at their brain. Mom can't smile because the awful background is giving her nausea, and Dad can't smile either because he's officially late for his tee time.

Some parting words of advice, Sears Portrait family: Stop buying hundreds of copies of these photos in various sizes. You only need three—one for Mom's fireplace, one for Grandma's fireplace, and one for Dad's wallet. Trust me—the rest are thrown away by relatives as soon as the Christmas card comes out of the envelope. Better yet, keep the photos that were in the wallet or picture frame when you bought it. Those people are better looking than anyone in your family will ever be.

Family Vacations

The term "family vacation" is an oxymoron. If you're stuck with your family, it ain't no vacation. We should call family vacations what they are: "Countdown to Dad's public tantrum."

Since Dad's guaranteed to blow a gasket, why not have fun with it? Push him right to the edge. Throw a fit until he buys you a $7 hamburger, take one bite, and say you're full. Wait until a mile after he's just pumped gas to have to pee. And, of course, side with Mom when she refuses to read the map but then help her bitch when he gets lost and refuses to ask for directions.

Family vacations are not vacations for anybody in the family. Fathers would rather be at work than actually dealing with their wife and kids. Mothers are mothers 24/7 no matter where they are, and children hate being stuck in a car for sixteen hours straight only to have to sleep three to a bed in a hotel.

When families stay with other relatives to save on the hotel bill, it always ends badly. Dad gets drunk and insults his sister-in-law while the children learn about sex and drugs from their older cousins.

Educational vacations are the worst. Museum curators speak slower than Gomer Pyle with peanut butter in his mouth. Hey, get to the point, bitch! Nobody cares where the fag who painted this grew up. The only thing museums are good for—one word: *air-conditioning*!

Disney World makes the kids happy, but it makes parents furious—furious they had to remortgage the house to stand in a three-hour line. Thank God Disney World is in Florida, where the sun puts people in an abnormally good mood. If it were in North Dakota, Disney World would be the murder-suicide capital of the world.

With all that being said, why do people go on family vacations? Because if they didn't, they'd just end up sitting at home bitching that they never go on vacation.

Child-rearing Books

Learning to raise a child from reading a book is like learning to swim from reading a book: You can't do it. You just have to jump in and *drown*.

It is a known fact that parents with the most parenting books suck the most. In parenting, you can't think; you have to react. How does some Jew with a bullshit degree know more about your child than you do? These books are usually written by some jack-off who doesn't even remember the names of the children from his first marriage.

Don't waste your time reading this stuff. During the time you're reading the stupid book, you could be reading to your kid or at least spending some quality time with him. Sure, you may pick up some tips in it, so just make the nanny or a grandparent read it in her downtime.

I've seen a ton of child-rearing books on conditioning your baby. They should all be called the same thing: *How to Shut Your Kid Up*. Hey, if you want to let your baby cry it out, that's fine—just don't do it on an airplane. If I wrote a child-rearing book, it would be called *Leave That Noisy Little Bastard at Home in a Drawer*.

My favorite child-rearing books are the ones all about love. They have titles like *How to Keep Your Baby Happy All the Time*. You can find those at most bookstores in the section marked "Fiction." If you really want to survive children without going nuts, let me recommend the book my parents read: *The Bartender's Guide to Mixed Drinks*.

Hot Babysitters

I am going to say something controversial here—*hire a hot babysitter*! Seriously, this is beneficial to your children. Hear me out. Studies show that people respond better to beautiful people. The children will be better behaved if your babysitter looks more like Hannah Montana and less like Ugly Betty. Your girls will want to act like big girls to impress the babysitter and your boys will be in their bedrooms quietly dreaming up *Penthouse Forum* fantasies.

Think of the alternative. An ugly babysitter will be a whore just to become popular. Therefore, you're liable to come home and hop into a bed of sticky sheets. Boy babysitters are just plain creepy. They're either sexual predators in waiting or cornholers, and either way, you don't want them near your loved ones.

I know what you're thinking: "Hey, Queen of Mean, what

if my babysitter is so hot my second husband can't help himself on the way home in the car?" All that means is that you should start working on husband number three.

"What about fat babysitters?" you might ask. Well, there are two schools of thought when it comes to the rotund teen. The downside is she may eat all of your food and there will be no Chunky Monkey left when you come home buzzed. There is an upside, however. You can always hire the kind of chubby bitch who cockblocks for the other girls at parties. Think about it: If she's willing to ruin her friends' fun, you know your kids aren't getting away with anything either.

Healthy Snacks

Parents, don't give your kids "healthy snacks." First of all, there are no such things as healthy snacks—there are just snacks that are less shitty for you. Every time you eat a snack, it's going to make your ass bigger, so you might as well enjoy it. People think fruit is a healthy snack, but fruit is full of sugar and citric acid that keeps you up all night eating Doritos. Low-fat and other "healthy" chips are made with chemicals that make you piss out of your asshole. How healthy can *that* be?

Foods that advertise they are healthy either have a serving size that wouldn't fill an Ethiopian infant or taste like shit. Low-calorie chocolate that tastes good is like sex with no strings attached—it doesn't exist. They say it's chocolate but it tastes like dirt and is drier than a camel's asshole. Rice cakes taste good if you put something fattening on them, but what's the point of that? Nuts are kind of healthy until you rip a hemorrhoid trying to send Mr. Peanut home. The worst health food is the pita. It turns every sandwich into a mess. That's why it's healthy—because you only get a third of the calories. The rest are on the floor.

A warning: Never spend time with parents who only let their kids have "healthy" snacks. You end up hating these people for no good reason. They hand their kid a bag of grapes, and you're like, "Oh, fuck you." It's the exact same reaction smokers have when cigarettes get banned from restaurants. One solution: Sneak those kids candy and soda when their parents aren't around. Just lure them by saying, "Come on, all the cool kids are doing it. One Oreo's not gonna kill you." We have to get the young people hooked, or in twenty years they'll ban junk food from bars and restaurants, and the next thing you know you'll have to sneak outside to eat a Ding Dong—which, by the way, is also code for "have gay Asian sex."

Sit, Kneel, Stand
• • • • • • • • • • •

The Virgin Mary

Some of you reading this may think the Virgin Mary is what your kids drink during brunch at Applebee's. However, the Virgin Mary is also the queen bee of the Catholic Church. In other words, her shit don't stink. In short, next to Oprah, she is the most influential woman in the world.

Mary is special because she is the mother of baby Jesus, and she had him without having sex. I know, I know . . . sounds impossible. But I did know a girl in college who went to sleep and woke up pregnant, so anything is possible. However, Mary was better because she became pregnant without the aid of Jäger bombs and fraternity brothers.

The Virgin Mary is relevant even all these years after baby Jesus's birth. For one thing, Mary would have made the best *Maury Povich* guest ever: "Find out who is Mary's baby daddy—Joseph or God—after the break." Italians love the Virgin Mary and play her song, "Ave Maria," at every Italian girl's first wedding. The Virgin Mary is also very important to Latinos. She has put millions of dollars into the Latin community around the world with her candles. Her candles light the way to the toilet for many a Latino with too much tequila in his belly. Virgin Mary tattoos are as popular with Latinos as over-the-ass tattoos are with whores. The Virgin Mary also brings the plight of Third World South American shitholes to American televisions when she appears in someone's stucco or tortilla and CNN shows up.

Due to Mary's significance, I can never understand why some people get upset when Catholics pray to her to get their message to God. As every guido knows, the easiest way to get someone to do something is to talk to his mother. Plus, Mary was Jewish, so you know she'll ride Jesus's ass until he gets the job done.

I think the time has come for Mary to be embraced by the black churches. If any group of people could understand a woman getting pregnant and not having the father around, it would be them.

Judaism and Other Inferior Religions

I'm tired of political correctness making us pretend that all religions are as good as Catholicism. It's obvious to me that they're not, and I don't even go to church anymore. I can just tell by the people I've been around.

Judaism is the original religion, based on original sin and original guilt. It is the *Godfather* of religions. It's for people who don't like sequels. Jews are called the chosen people because they said so and, hey, they control everything, or at least everything important, like the banks, the government, and the media, so they must be right. Judaism is an old religion and many people have tried in vain to kill it off, but it will never go away as long as people still want to make it in Hollywood. Plus, Judaism is not a giving religion. Jews are selfish—if they weren't, they'd tip more and get male enhancement surgery.

Islam is the *Godfather: Part III* of religions, universally panned as awful. Islam is a religion for smelly Arabs and for blacks who are either uppity or who have gone to prison. Islam makes black people change their name to something even more ridiculous. People who believe in Islam don't believe in Jesus or deodorant. They don't let their women drive or look good, so they have to wrap them up in blankets to have sex with them. Because they don't drink alcohol, the less they see of each other the better. Islamics who live in the Middle East hate the Jews more than Mel Gibson and Hitler combined because the Jews have the only beachfront property in that godforsaken wasteland. In America, Muslims wear itchy beards and crazy hats. They're basically pissed-off Amish who drive cabs.

Asians have a bunch of wacky religions. One is called Buddhism, where they pray to a fat man named Buddha. How ironic! Skinny people praying to a fat god. Buddha has more idiotic sayings than Yogi Berra, but they're in Chinese, so nobody cares.

Dot Indians believe in reincarnation, which means you come back to life as different animals, so your bacon cheeseburger was really your great-grandfather with your cousin who died at birth on top. Hindus are evil because if they loved their neighbors, they'd stop making the entire apartment complex stink of curry.

Finally, if you want to make it in Hollywood and do not look like a Jew but have just as much money, you can join Scientology. This helps you in the business, but unfortunately, it also makes you gay.

Birth Control

I don't understand the Catholic Church's stance on birth control. It says the pill and condoms are wrong, but the man is allowed to pull out. Apparently, birth control is only a sin when it doesn't stain your sheets.

Birth control is a very big deal to me because I bang the blacks and don't want to be a single mom. Some people think taking it in the poop chute is birth control because the alternative—getting it all over your boobs—is just plain messy. In the face is never an alternative for me because of how long it takes to do my hair.

There are many forms of birth control. I do not approve of condoms. They break and they taste funny. Men never carry them, and after a trip to the drugstore, the buzz from the Riunite has usually worn off.

There is a device called an IUD, which is a fishhook in your vag. It hooks the egg like a trout. It's like your own *Deadliest Catch*. There are dams you can stick up your hole, but when you're with a black man, there isn't any room to spare up there. And if you bang a Latino, they just jimmy the lock and get in there anyway.

The easiest birth control to deal with is the pill. It makes you fat and bitchy, which is a natural birth control in itself. For the truly lazy out there, there is abortion, but it is dangerous because you might get beaten over the head with a picket sign on your way into the clinic.

The Pope Visits America

The Pope coming to America is a big waste of money. Hey, Father! We already have the book, we don't need the fairy tale read to us.

The Pope is basically a hypocrite. He forgives every child-molesting priest he can swing his gay-ass cane at, but a poor single mom is going to hell for having an abortion. Yeah, that makes sense. And he bitches about how violent a country we are, but he has no idea. I say we take away his security and let him walk through New York with all that gaudy jewelry on, and he can see just how violent we *really* are.

All this guy does is complain about how evil America is and we cheer him on. It's like taking your mother-in-law to brunch and listening to her gripe about what a terrible person you are. Fuck him and his Popemobile!

When the Pope comes to America, we treat him like he won the Super Bowl. It's like the Beatles landed at JFK when he hits American soil. It's less like a religious experience and more like a rock show. He comes out in his Elvis jumpsuit and big hat, and his opening act is some cardinal that nobody cares about. A bunch of priests run around like roadies, getting the stage ready and finding crippled groupies for him to heal. After the show, the Pope signs autographs and has his picture taken with people. The only difference between the Pope and U2 is that the Pope is less preachy than Bono and easier to understand.

Priests Who Wear Shorts

I find something off-putting about a priest who wears shorts. And I don't mean if he's playing basketball. I mean black shorts with his black shirt and white collar. What are we supposed to think about that? "Is that our priest or do we have a really religious mailman?" Bad enough his legs are whiter than Frosty the Snowman's junk—up against those black shorts, they're transparent! The only thing nastier than a priest's legs is a nun's mustache.

And why are priests showing us their legs in the first place? It's bad enough they nicked the collection basket for a gym membership; now they have to show us they've been working on their calves while they should be working on our salvation. "Who's that with the sexy calves? Father Jerry. Oooh."

What's the point of a priest wearing shorts anyway? Christ died for your sins, Father, and you can't take a little heat? Don't his pasty legs stick to the leather interior of his Lincoln Continental? Is he trying to look good, and for *whom*? Hey, Father, if you want to fool around with broads, just become a Protestant minister. They get all the bitches.

One word of warning, priests: If we can see your legs, then we're just inches away from your nuts peeking out. And I was taught if you stare into a priest's scrotum, you turn into a pillar of salt. And to that I say, "No, thanks."

What Would Jesus Do?

"What Would Jesus Do?" bracelets were very popular a few years back. If you're unfamiliar with them, the WWJD bracelet is supposed to work like a dog's choke chain, making you stop and think before you sin. But just as a dog's neck gets stronger, so does your ability to carry guilt, thereby lessening the bracelet's effectiveness.

I would be lying if I said the feminist cunt in me doesn't react by saying, "Why do we have to listen to a man for everything?" Seriously, does Jesus know how many tampons to put in your purse? Does Jesus know which Asian does the best job of waxing my junk?

And besides, Jesus isn't always right. Sometimes being a doormat isn't the answer. In some instances, the saying should be "What Would the Rock Do?" Unfortunately, more often than not, the answer would be "A shitty movie."

I just don't understand why people wear the "What Would Jesus Do?" bracelets if they're not going to pay attention to them. I met a guy in a bar wearing a WWJD bracelet. Well, for starters, Mac, I don't think Jesus'd order a Jack and Coke. He was always more of a wine guy. And if Jesus *did* order a Jack and Coke, I don't think he'd send it back if it was watered down.

Then Mr. WWJD hit on me—which was fine, but he only did it after he had clearly exhausted his other options at the bar. I think Jesus would have been a little classier than that. As a matter of fact, he might have even started with the heavier girls in a charitable kind of way. This moron probably also had one of those little Christian fish on the back of the car that he was going to drive home drunk in later.

People, Christianity isn't a membership card to Blockbuster Video—either you're in or you're out. If you're out, take off the bracelet, and if you're in, quite honestly, take off the bracelet if you're trying to score chicks at nightclubs. Because I don't know what Jesus would do, but I know what Lisa would do, and it ain't you.

Confession

Confession is the best thing about being Catholic. Confession enables you to wipe away all of your sins simply by telling them to the right person. You go into a room the size of a coat check and bare your soul to an alcoholic pedophile to guarantee your entrance into heaven. You don't even have to show your face to the priest, which makes this very easy. I always thought it would be great to be a nasty whore your whole life then get a final confession on your deathbed. It sounds great on paper until you unexpectedly get hit by a bus, don't have the time to apologize, and spend the rest of eternity sucking on Hitler's little cock.

After you tell the priest all of your sins, he gives you a punishment. I never figured out the equation. For example, is masturbation five or ten Hail Marys? Sometimes the priest gives you a punishment like "I want you to try to make better decisions next time." Those are the best! Hey, Father Dopey, you just let me off the hook without making me get on my knees and pray. Cool! My knees won't be sore the next time I sin.

Some people get bent out of shape about Catholics confessing their sins to a priest. They say, "Why not just confess them straight to God? Why go through a middleman?" Well, for starters, God forgives all sins, so if it wasn't for the priests, we'd have no one to make us feel guilty. Sure, God will forgive you if you sleep with that drunk brother from the club, but what's to keep you from doing it again? Only when you tell the elderly gentleman who baptized you as a baby that you bought a man drinks all night just so he would let you pipe him in an alley while his friends took photos with their phones do you really start to see the error of your ways. Only when your priest excuses himself to barf do you start to understand the destructive power of sin and the visual images of the words "rim job from a blind guy." If you sin before God, you feel guilty, but that feeling goes away. But if your priest gives you a penance of three rosaries and a visit to the Department of Health, you really do start to walk the straight and narrow. The spirit is willing, but the flesh is weak, and at no time is that more evident than when a sixty-five-year-old celibate asks you to explain what you meant when you said "teabag."

School Daze, or I'll Have an Honor Roll with Extra Jelly, Please

Girl Scout Cookies
Girl Scout cookies are evil. Not only do they have all the temptation of a regular cookie, they come with the self-satisfying feeling that you're helping some little girl go to camp. This is like your crack dealer having a scholarship fund.

The names of the cookies are very confusing. This is a carefully designed system devised to make you buy more than one box because every year you forget which ones you like and which ones you hate. Therefore, Girl Scout cookies contribute to America's growing obesity problem. They're little fat bullets filled with more chemicals than Artie Lange's body. Girl Scout cookies are so indestructible they'll be what the cockroaches eat after World War III.

Gym Class vs. the Fat Kids

Gym class is as hard on the fat kid as math class is on the black kid. Gym class was invented to tire kids out so they wouldn't be hyper in science class. This isn't necessary for the fat kids—they get tired standing up for the Pledge of Allegiance.

Now, don't get me wrong: Gym class is useful for several reasons. First, it's the only time stupid kids—I mean jocks—get to feel superior in school. Gym also gives football coaches a class they can teach besides study hall and driver's ed. And it gives football players an A to help their grades.

However, gym class is evil because it is God's way of punishing kids for being fat. It's the only possible explanation. First, you are humiliated by wearing shorts specially made to crawl up the crack of your fat ass. Then you spend the next hour being beaten by large rubber balls thrown at your fat gut that your fat little legs are too slow to run from. Then, of course, is the pièce de résistance—the shower. Being fat, you obviously got sweaty, so now you have to choose—stink the rest of the day or have your friends gag at the sight of your stretch marks.

On the upside, though, gym is the first time many students

experience lesbianism—even if it is just the girls' volleyball coach's haircut.

Homeschooling

Homeschooling is the worst thing you can do to kids short of raping them. School is about learning how to deal with others, not seeing what level the little prick can read at. Who cares how smart you are if you can't properly interact with others? How is your son going to be prepared for the rigors of corporate America if he is not constantly being beaten up during recess and given swirlies after school? And how do you expect your daughters to ever have healthy relationships as adults if they are not being ridiculed for their appearance in middle school? Unless you want your kid to work at the underground Biosphere, send him to school.

Besides, what can children learn at home that they can't learn at school? That Mommy likes her Xanax? Sure, you may be able to teach your children math and English better than some burned-out lifer who doesn't give a shit, but who's going to teach them about sex and drugs? Those conversations are very awkward in the home and are best handled by kids in the schoolyard.

Some parents keep their kids at home for religious reasons. But you know what they say: Those who don't believe in evolution haven't been touched by it. If you don't send your kids to school, they have to learn about the world from television. I know your local minister/thief may not want you to believe this, but there's more sex and violence on *Jerry Springer* than in English class. How long are you going to shelter the kid?

Forever? Is he going to work from home making millions stuffing envelopes?

Quite honestly, our entire economic system is based on people succeeding just to stick it up the ass of people who were mean to them in high school. So homeschooling is jeopardizing our entire economy—not to mention creating some weird little fucks.

SATs

SATs are tests given to high school kids designed to ruin their lives, or at least one of their Saturdays. Colleges supposedly use them to judge prospective students, therefore everyone takes these tests way too seriously.

Students who take the SATs are set up to fail from the beginning. First of all, no one performs well on Saturday mornings except Scooby-Doo and horny scout leaders. By the time most students' hangovers have worn off, the test is over and their scores are so bad they might as well drive right over to the local community college.

Critics say the test is culturally biased against blacks and Latinos, and to that I say, "Of course it is." Students use number-two pencils to fill in the holes. To make things unbiased, they should let the blacks shoot holes in the tests and let Latinos stab them.

Standardized tests are all a farce. The SAT shows only two things: that students who score well A) know words that make them look like assholes when they use them, and B) know how to solve math problems they'll never need unless they're Asian.

If this country really wants to see how well students will do in college, they should get the kids drunk, stoned, and laid and see if they can still show up the next morning for a nine A.M. class without their mom driving them. Now, *that's* a test!

Guidance Counselors

Anyone who listens to a guidance counselor is a fool. All guidance counselors want to do is talk you out of your dream because they never achieved theirs. Trust me—every guidance counselor hates his job, because talking to zit-faced seventeen-year-olds has never been anybody's dream.

Guidance counselors are only guidance counselors because they flunked out of grad school. The only thing your guidance counselor cares about is if he can see down your shirt while you're filling out his stupid questionnaire.

Counselors love to think the worst of each student. Seriously, they must get kickbacks from DeVry, because that's where they want to send everyone. Another one of their favorite suggestions is the police academy. Guidance counselors direct so many students to the police academy because they want to know every cop when they get pulled over for drunk driving after they've drowned their own career sorrows.

Come to think of it, has there ever been a more worthless position than high school guidance counselor? These people are paid to say things like "If you want to go to college, you better take college prep classes." No shit. You mean Harvard's not going to care that I just made a killer spice rack in shop? Here is a quote you will never hear in a presidential inauguration speech: "I would like to thank my high school guidance counselor . . . because without him, my life would have turned out *exactly the same*!"

Guidance counselors are essentially human resources people who don't want to work in the summer. And no one calls them on their bullshit! I mean, who's going back to high school to tell their counselor off when they have so many burgers to flip? They tell students things like "Nobody makes it in Hollywood." Hey, if I want that kind of discouragement, I'll listen to my parents.

People Who Take High School Sports Too Seriously

Is there a bigger bunch of losers out there than people who take high school sports seriously? Yes! People who take T-ball seriously.

High school students are under enough pressure; sports should not add to it. Kids in high school should be lighting farts and fingerbanging. People who rely on fifteen-year-old athletes to get their rocks off need better cable.

Parents, hear my plea: Don't be so proud your kid is on the football team. He does drugs too. And townspeople who never made it to college, lighten up! You care way too much because high school was the last time you were cool. The athletes care because they think if they're good, they'll get a scholarship to college and do well in life. That ain't necessarily so: You want to find some famous former high school athletes? Just go to the mall. They're working as security guards.

In general, everyone involved should remember that winning a high school football game is just that—winning a *game*. It doesn't really prove that the other town sucks! And if you really want to bore the shit out of someone, start telling the story of how you scored the winning basket twenty years ago. "Wow! Tell me more! Did you get to boff a cheerleader after?" Nobody cares. And let's face it—if you had gone to a high school that had black kids, you wouldn't have made the team to begin with.

Yearbook Signing

Yearbooks and dry humping are the two things nobody wants to think about after high school. Yearbooks are a reminder of either what a geek you were or what a loser you've become. The school's pretty girls got married early, became impregnated, and were left for a younger secretary. Jocks got fat and they're still stupid. And the math geek who's now an engineer has hired the jock to mow his lawn. It's one case of hilarious karmic retribution after another.

The worst part of the yearbook is the photos. Your yearbook photo only comes in handy twice in your adult life—either for your VH1 *Behind the Music* or E! *True Hollywood Story,* or when you commit a heinous crime and the yearbook photo is the only one they have to show on the news.

And the sentiments written in yearbooks! They last just about as long as the keg at the graduation party. "Best Friends Forever" lasts until the first week of college when you meet ten girls who are cooler than your high school BFF, who's now enrolled in beauty school. "Have a great summer" really meant "Don't sleep with my boyfriend or get pregnant." And "Never change" meant "I hope to always be better than you."

I think people shouldn't sign yearbooks until their twenty-year high school reunion. The sayings would be much more realistic. I'd love to crack open a yearbook and read "You were a lot cockier when you had hair," "Minivan or miniskirt. You can't have both," and "Please don't tell my husband we had sex." And of course, my personal favorite: "I wouldn't have teased you so much if I had known you would someday own Microsoft."

Part Three: Comedian, Heal Thyself! . . . Comedy's Lovable Queen of Denial

. . . .

Addictions

People think the only bad addictions in life are drugs and alcohol. But people are addicted to almost everything and don't even know it. They're hooked on approval, shopping, porn. Porn is definitely a big one. If your favorite computer file contains anything with the words "hot," "horny," or "high school," then you are definitely addicted to porn. And if you've ever Googled the words "dirty sanchez" on your work computer, you better seek help. Put it this way: If you're looking for a job, it's much better to say you left your last one over money issues as opposed to having an insatiable foot fetish.

Some addictions are harder to identify than others. Is someone a sex addict or is that less a disease and more a subtle way for guys to brag? Some people are blind to their addictions. I once saw a 350-pound man mocking crack addicts. That's right, sir, they're weak-minded pieces of shit. Now keep eating pizza and cake until your knees give out or your heart explodes, whichever comes first.

Some people are addicted to TV—of course, it's never PBS, it's always the TV equivalent of crack, i.e., soap operas or the news. People addicted to soaps live in a fantasy world. They wait in their trailer for their long-lost stepbrother to make them president of his oil empire. On the other hand, people addicted to news live their lives in fear and shoot the paperboy when he shows up an hour early. Some people are even addicted to crossword puzzles or Sudoku. For those of you who don't know, Sudoku is the gook crossword puzzle with numbers. Gooks can't handle regular crossword puzzles because their culture doesn't use words, it uses pictures, like a fucked-up game of Concentration.

Some people are addicted to exercise. These people think if they jog far enough, they'll never die. No, Jim Fixx, it means you'll probably get hit by a car driven by someone who's addicted to something a little easier on the knees. The worst addiction of all is religion. It makes you a self-righteous asshole and it might all be for nothing if there's no God anyway. At least when you're addicted to food, the Lord is right there stuffed inside a jelly doughnut.

Interventions

Interventions are a great way to lose a friend. That is because people don't want to hear the truth about themselves. Addicts know they have a problem. Interventions are as bad as telling someone her boyfriend is cheating on her. Let her find out on her own. Remember: They always shoot the messenger.

Interventions are like baby showers—nobody wants to attend them but they're forced to go. But instead of getting you gifts, your friends and family sit around and tell you what a fuckup you are. If you're ever tempted to throw an intervention, have some balls and talk to the person in private yourself. If he won't listen to you personally, fuck 'im. Bringing more people into the mix just spreads the drama, and everybody has enough drama. People only change because they want to or have to, not because someone bought a deli tray.

Most of the time, an intervention happens because someone is a drunk or on drugs, and everyone tells the person how he has hurt them while taking the drugs. If your friends are trying an intervention with you because of drugs or alcohol, my advice would be to deny you have a problem, scream "Fuck you!", and then leave. It's really doing them a favor, because they'll have a much better story to tell their friends. If you just sit there and say, "You know what? You're right. I need help," that's a real snore. Your friends went through the trouble of ganging up on you, and your acquiescence is a real buzzkill for them. Also, when they cart you off to rehab, don't just go. Go kicking and screaming. Again, it will make your friends feel better about their efforts. After all, your drinking has been a huge pain in their ass—don't you at least owe them a good story?

I think people should conduct interventions in cases other than drinking or drugging. They should do an intervention if someone is a dick. That's a great intervention because there's nothing to blame the guest of honor's behavior on other than the fact that he's an asshole. A word of advice, however: If anyone ever does an intervention on you like that, just blame your dad and start crying. You'll get out of there in fifteen minutes tops. But only do this if your parents aren't there. Otherwise, you're in for two hours minimum.

Codependence

Everyone is codependent to a certain degree. Be it on a dog, a talk-show host, or a puppet, everyone is dependent on something. The dog is man's best friend because some people can only be friends with things with worse breath than them. Cats exist because some people are so lonely, they'll pretend a cat gives a shit about them.

Psychologists say that codependents are people who care "too much" for someone who depends on them. That is why we codependents prefer fuckups—because they need us. We actually are attracted to the nonfun part of alcoholics. Screw the parties and the socializing. Give me the vomiting and unemployment. If you're broke and smell like puke, you're not going to leave me for a younger woman. Essentially, the codependent's motto is "I would rather be miserable than be alone." Unless, of course, it's during sex.

Here are some symptoms of codependents: We are constantly lying for the other person, saying he's sick instead of saying he's hungover or, even more accurately, at the dry cleaners trying to get the piss stain out of the couch cushion. We make excuses for the person: "He's not a homo. He's just too drunk to get it up," or, as we like to call it, the Liza Minnelli defense. Codependents also have problems with intimacy, but that's hard to prove since the people we date are usually drunk, stoned, or whacking off to freaky porn.

Some people don't think codependency is a disease. Those are the same people who cruise AA meetings like they're singles bars and get pissed off whenever the word "rehab" is brought up. If you've ever taken back a boyfriend who has habitually cheated on you because he said he would "die without you," you are not well and you should seek help. So join me. I know this great AA meeting with a ton of hot single guys.

Love at First Sight vs. Being Friends First

I don't believe in love at first sight, but I do believe in lust at first sight. Everybody has lust at first sight. Then the hard body talks and you want to suck the juice back up your leg. I see tons of men for the first second and I want to fuck them. But one minute later, I find ten things that turn me off about them, like the fact that they're wearing sandals or live in Cleveland. I'll still fuck them, but there's no love involved. Most love-at-first-sight relationships end in "I'll kill that son of a bitch the next time I see him." You see stars going in and you want him to see stars on the way out.

On the other hand, it's easy to sleep with a friend because there are lots of opportunities to do so: a mutual friend's party, running into them at the store, you're drunk and don't have cab fare. Being friends with someone before you get involved means you may lose their friendship when it's over, but, hey, I lose friends like stoners lose their keys. Just go for it.

The question is: Do you want the fire of love at first sight or the security of being friends first? That's like saying, which is more important—the sex or the conversation? When you're young, it's definitely the sex. Let's face it, everybody's single, you have lots of friends to talk to, and your hormones are so crazy you're faking yeast infections just to have an excuse to scratch.

But picking someone just because they are attractive makes as much sense as a dog picking its mate by sniffing her ass. It can get you stuck with someone you hate just because they gave you a little tail. That's why creatures that mate for life tend to all look exactly the same, like penguins or Asians.

The problem with love at first sight is that the dating relationship is very different from the marriage relationship, which is completely different from the parenting relationship. It's better to have boring sex with a friend and responsible spouse than exciting sex with a douchebag. And if you don't think that's true, you haven't been following Britney Spears lately.

Online Flirting/Cheating

Checking people out online is not cheating any more than checking people out at the mall is cheating. However, if you're in a relationship and *meeting* people on the web, you're just like every other degenerate fuck in the universe. Turn off the computer and love the one you're with. Remember, the grass is always greener when you don't have to listen to them talk. Fucking someone you met online in a seedy hotel room is cheating.

If you're single, communicating with strangers on the Internet is a great way to meet a lot of people. People don't connect in bars anymore and meeting at the gym is so 1988. People flirt on the web because single moms can't leave their kids at home and troll for dad number two at the bar, and men can't get their third DUI waiting for Miss Close Enough. If you're single, cruising for people on the web is a great way to save gas and the environment.

The Internet, however, has complicated being in a relationship. It used to be if you feared your boyfriend cheating, you kept him home. Nowadays, that's the worst place he could be. At least in public, he only flirts with women who are attractive, and the losers I date don't get too far with that type. But online flirting is unstoppable. One minute, your boyfriend tells you he wants to check the score of the game, and five minutes later, you walk in on him whacking off. "Uh, I'm guessing the Knicks finally won a game?"

Texting While on Dates

Texting on a date is completely inappropriate unless it's a blind date, and by "blind date," I mean the other person is blind. What could be more important on a date with me than *me*? Texting has become something everyone accepts people doing. I had a guy trying to text someone while I was blowing him. He asked me what button makes the smiley face and I said, "The one I'm sucking on."

Texting has gotten way out of hand. Everyone is texting constantly and no one is that important or interesting. I understand texting at an airport or in a doctor's office, but if you're that bored on a date, buy your own dinner and masturbate. I'm not saying you can't peek at your phone to see if someone hotter or with more money wants a shot at you, but typing away like a coked-out Stephen King is just plain rude. Quite honestly, the only way your fingers should be working that hard on a date is if your hands are under the table and up my skirt. There's only one acceptable text to send while on a date and it reads, "I'm gonna fuck him :)."

Remember when the most obnoxious behavior on a date was when the guy chewed with his mouth open? Those were the good ol' days before cell phones. I don't know which is worse—the fact that they are sending messages to someone else during dinner or the fact that they only look up long enough to check out the waitress's ass.

And what could possibly be so important that it can't wait

until after the date? I mean, sure, your friends want to know if UROK. And if you are enjoying your DNR. And if this date could be a possible LTR. But we are on a D8. And I don't care if your friends are drunk at a bar, which is always good for an LOL, but they need to say TTFN, and they can T2UL8R. Either that or tonight you ain't getting NUFN.

Maintaining Contact with Exes and Former Fuck Buddies

Remaining friends with someone you have been romantically involved with depends on two things: How close were you before you got together, and how did it end? If it ended with the words "cunt" and "worthless nigger," you're probably not gonna be meeting for coffee on a rainy Saturday.

It's hard for two people to stay friends if one of the parties wants to remain a couple or has no other options. If you can have an emotionless booty call after the breakup, more power to you. But in most cases to remain friends, you need to have an activity you enjoy together that doesn't involve jizz, like the Yankees or the opera.

Sometimes you can stay good friends until one of you meets the One. Once people meet the One, all old exes and fuck buddies need to go out the window. No guy wants to hang out with someone who used to shoot loads on his girl. Girls have a hard time being friends with any girl the guy knows for fear of getting too close to the enemy. Sometimes it's impossible to hang out with people after you have had sex with them because you can't look them in the eye knowing they like it in the ass too.

Quite frankly, why would you possibly want to stay friends with your ex? Either you didn't get along or he dumped you for someone better looking. If that's the case, why should you hang out with the shallow prick to begin with? That would be like eating at a restaurant that fired you. Why give them the extra business when it would be much more fun to spread rumors that they masturbate in the soup? Which, by the way, is the rumor I used to spread about all my ex-boyfriends until one told me he only did that once because he ran out of salt.

Fat Girl, Interrupted

. . . .

Affirmations

Affirmations are little sayings losers repeat to trick themselves into feeling good about themselves. I like to call this "psychology for dummies." Sayings like "You can do it" and "Everybody likes you" make T-ball rewarding but do absolutely nothing in adulthood. Affirmations actually make people feel worse about themselves, because deep down inside they know that the affirmations are not true. If you have to tell yourself you're pretty, trust me, you're not. Everyone knows that when it comes to beauty, the only opinions that count are the opinions of others. If no one has ever bought you a drink in a bar, you better write "I'm pretty" in lipstick on the mirror big enough to cover your whole face because, believe it, you are fucking ugly.

Maybe I'm just too smart to fool myself, but how can repeating something a hundred times make it so? If the theory behind affirmations is true, I guess O. J. wrote "I didn't kill that white bitch and that little Hebe" on his hand every day before he went into the courtroom.

The best way to stop hating yourself isn't to repeat gibber-ish you know isn't true all day long. The secret is to just stop thinking about yourself and turn your attention to others. To that end, do affirmations but choose ones that show how good you are in comparison to other, less fortunate people. For example, replace the negative thought "I'm a fat pig" with the positive sentiment "I am a sexy bitch, at least compared to these other cows shopping at Lane Bryant." When you take the time to see how much more awful other people are, you'll start to feel much better about you. Pretty soon, you'll stop chanting, "I am perfect just the way I am," and start chanting, "Well, at least I'm not as fucked up as Julie," which is all we really want anyway, right? To be less fucked up than our peers.

Fat Self-helpers

Oprah is the biggest fraud on television. She is always telling other people to stay true to themselves, but if she was true to herself, she'd be fingerbanging Gayle onstage every show instead of listening to what Dr. Oz says about vegetables. As if she cares about healthy food! Oprah eats vegetables about as much as I eat pussy.

Oprah pretends to care about other people, but she has more money than God and only gives it to that child abuse camp in Africa. That's like calling yourself a great humani-tarian because for less than the price of a cup of coffee you sponsor a kid in the jungle. Oprah also acts like she gives a shit about her guests' problems. I haven't seen someone fake cry that well since I told my mother I was breaking up with my spoon boyfriend. But people are fooled by Oprah's phony sympathy because of her acting ability. That bitch must imagine someone ate her last piece of cheesecake to conjure up that kind of emotion.

The second biggest fraud on TV is Oprah's friend Dr. Phil. The first time I saw Dr. Phil's show, I thought it was a *Mad TV* sketch, because it's too funny for *Saturday Night Live*. Dr. Dre is a more legitimate doctor than Dr. Phil. Dr. Phil is more full of shit than a Porta Potty at a rib fest. It never ceases to amaze me that people take life advice from a guy who's on after *Guiding Light*.

Wake up, people! Dr. Phil spells "prophet" P-R-O-F-I-T. That man will put a book on the shelves about anything, even weight loss. What kind of balls does it take for a fat ass like Dr. Phil to have weight-loss books? The man has no shame. What's next? The Dr. Phil Hair Restoration System?

By the way, if my editor deletes this rant, I would be happy to be part of Oprah's Book Club.

Smartwater

Let me get this out of the way right from the start. Drinking Smartwater does not make you smarter. Seriously, if water made you smarter, the government would never let it out, like the cure for AIDS. Our government wants people dumb enough to pay four dollars a gallon for gas, not people smart enough to start a revolution.

Anybody who buys bottled water is, by definition, stupid. Water used to be free. Now we idiots pay two dollars a bottle and have the balls to name it Smartwater. If we were smart, we'd drink water from the faucet. Smartwater's manufacturers say it's called Smartwater because it has electrolytes and vitamins added, unlike tap water, which has lead, copper, and sewage added. And what is an electrolyte anyway? I think it's just a fancy way of saying "calorie." No wonder everyone in this country is obese. We've even found a way to make our water fattening. What's next? Fudge-flavored air? Trust me, my dad invented that years ago.

Smartwater is also proof of how pretentious we are. "Do you drink water?" "Of course not! What am I—a Mexican? I drink Smartwater." And you can tell that Smartwater is for intelligent people, because their spokesperson is Jennifer Aniston. Yes, I immediately think intelligence whenever I see *her*. What happened? Was Jessica Simpson not available? Was Pam Anderson too busy with her "I'll suck the cock of every white trash rock star, but I won't eat meat" campaign? And what "smart" activity do they have Jennifer Aniston doing in the ad? Sitting naked right behind the bottle, just to drive the point home in case you didn't notice that the bottle is shaped like a dildo. Great campaign, guys! Calling a product "smart" and then advertising it in the most obvious, mindless way. I guess that's what you get when your marketing team is the Hilton sisters.

Vegetarians, Vegans, and Other Wastes of Skin

Vegetarians are the most annoying people on earth because these cunts are always hungry. What they don't know is if they just ate a piece of meat, their bellies would be full and they could quit whining. Vegetarians are not just annoying—they're stupid, because you need protein to maintain your brain and a fake hamburger doesn't have enough protein.

Some people are vegetarians because they say they want to

be healthy, but then they end up eating Snickers bars for dinner because "it's not meat." That kind of diet may keep some of them skinny, but it also gives them a deathly shade of gray. Some people are vegetarian because they think eating meat is cruel to animals. Yeah, right—like animals aren't mean?!? Every animal on earth would gnaw you down to your fake fingernails and breast implants if you came between it and its survival. Hell, Lassie would chow on little Timmy if they ran out of Alpo. And cruelty! Who cares? Steaks are so delicious, they're well worth the "pain" of the slaughterhouse. Besides, cows are the fat chicks of animals. They'll let anyone play with their titties. There deserves to be a little thinning of the herd.

Vegetarians especially hate veal because the meat comes from baby animals. Screw you, hippies! I love veal. In fact, I personally want to thank all the farmers out there for getting up at four in the morning, putting on the glove, and sticking it in through the cage to massage the baby calves.

If you're going to be a vegetarian, do me a favor. Don't pretend it's mainstream and expect me to bend over backward for you. There are more people in this country who smoke cigarettes than people who don't eat meat. We won't allow cigarette smokers to light up in a restaurant, so why do you think we'll give a shit that you're offended that our pasta sauce has meat?

Vegans are a whole other level of vegetarian asshole. These retards don't even drink real milk—they drink that gook milk. They say humans are the only adult animal that drinks milk. Well, no shit. We're the only ones who are able to milk a cow. Adult cats go crazy for milk when you give it to them. But they get kicked in the head when they try to milk the cow themselves.

And talk about emaciated! Vegans look like their skin is going to fall off their brittle little bones. And their personalities are no better! Hanging out with those lifeless shitheads is about as fun as eating their tasteless cookies.

I do agree with one thing the vegans do, however: not wearing leather. I never wear leather—not because it's cruel, but because it makes my twat sweat.

Deepak Chopra

Deepak Chopra is a nut job doctor from India who decided to start writing books after going into the emergency rooms and having dying patients tell him they wanted to wait for the white doctor, or at least a Chink. The guy has written more books than Stephen King and they make as much sense as Pink Floyd lyrics.

Chopra claims God is not an old man in heaven, he is a spirit who lives in every person. This guy must not watch National Geographic Channel's *Inside Maximum Security*. Chopra's hippie bullshit is why this country is fucked. Most people don't need a hug—they need to get kicked in the fucking head.

In his defense, Deepak Chopra is the one Indian who Americans will actually listen to. And he didn't even change his name to Steve or Mike like those fake-ass Indians you have to talk to when you call the HP computer help desk. Chopra is one of these spiritual freaks, like your yoga teacher, who think everything can be solved with a better understanding of the mind-and-body connection. Cancer, world peace, the Yankees' pitching—everything can be healed with meditation. In fact, he thinks meditation and self-awareness are the primary factors in getting sick and getting well. At least that's what he tells his nurses when he doesn't want to use a condom.

In some ways, I have to agree with Chopra. My doctor is always asking me stupid questions, like does my family have a history of cancer or heart disease, and do I exercise and watch what I eat. Instead, Chopra would just ask me if I was meditating on my health. Yes, I meditate on my health for thirty minutes every morning. I know it's thirty minutes, because I do it while I'm taking a shit.

Celebrity Rehab

Nowadays, rehab is the latest implement in the celebrity's career toolbox. If a celeb can't flash her gash getting out of a car or adopt a Pygmy, she goes to rehab and those flashbulbs start a-poppin'. Real-life people go to rehab after a lifetime of mistakes. Celebrities go after one, just to get on *Access Hollywood*. Celebrity rehab is what you do when you want to save your career and you're not good-looking enough to sleep with a producer.

Celebrity rehab has become just another way to promote a project. "Let's see . . . I could fly around the country doing interviews or I could skip it, go to rehab, and get twice as much press. Sign me up!"

And celebrities will use any excuse in the book to go to rehab. Instead of just admitting they have a problem with Jews or blacks, they pretend they have a problem with drugs and alcohol. But thankfully, they get what's coming to them. These big shots go to rehab thinking they're going to be treated like stars and that they're going to have to sign autographs, then they get there and they're treated like every other loser. They should know better. People trying to kick heroin don't care about your movie career. They just don't want to shit their pants at night when they get strapped into a bed.

Celebrity rehab is like putting violent criminals together in jail. They keep themselves busy making new contacts for when they get released. Forget MySpace. If you want to network, get into celebrity rehab. You'll come out with a new agent and a new manager, and Steven Tyler will offer to do the soundtrack on your next movie. Twenty-eight days later, you come out on the A list with three movie offers and a complimentary date with Jennifer Aniston. As a matter of fact, celebrity rehab is so important to a career in show business that a star's drug dealer is now a legitimate tax write-off under the category of Ridiculous Bullshit Expenses, like plastic surgery or a publicist.

"Kumbaya"

"Kumbaya" is a song that was written before music was used as a form of entertainment. The song became famous in the thirties and has all of the joy and hope of the Great Depression. In the sixties, "Kumbaya" was sung by that downer cunt Joan Baez, so you know it has all the musical finesse of a retard banging his head against the wall.

"Kumbaya" is a song drenched in naïveté. It's sung by enemies who still hate each other but want the photo op. It's sung in rehab when you leave to push you out the door with positivity. This is hypocritical, because your fellow rehabbers want you to die a painful death and the rehab center wants you to come back and give them more money. It's the same fake nice you get at the supermarket or the bank because they have to give you a toaster if they don't smile.

When it was written, "Kumbaya" was a heartfelt spiritual song. Today if you are singing "Kumbaya," it means you have made some horrible error in life, like getting addicted to drugs or signing up for summer camp. The song is supposed to be about inviting Jesus into your life. Instead, it's being sung by some horny white guy with a Jew-fro trying to seem sensitive just so he can get into some vulnerable girl's pants. And they always make you hold hands and sing it around a campfire in the middle of the woods. That's why we've never found Bigfoot. His only experience with human beings is hunters, gay men cornholing in the woods, or former druggies singing a cheesy song whose name means "douchebag with a guitar."

Twenty-eight Days

Twenty-eight days is how long they keep you in rehab, unless you're a celebrity who can leave whenever there are enough paparazzi outside.

When you're in rehab, twenty-eight days seems an eternity. It feels longer than Tommy Lee's dick. To put it in perspective, think about it: In twenty-eight days, you can watch 1,344 episodes of *Two and a Half Men* and still not laugh once. In twenty-eight days, someone would finally kill Jack Bauer. And it *does* change you. After twenty-eight days, I forgot what my car looked like in the parking lot. If you think you can do twenty-eight days in rehab, try not going to the bathroom for twenty-eight days. It's that uncomfortable and you're that up to your elbows in shit.

Twenty-eight days is not only how long most addicts stay in treatment, twenty-eight days is also how long Black History Month lasts. So, apparently, twenty-eight days is the length of time we can pretend to give a shit about something we really aren't that into.

Twenty-eight days is supposed to be four weeks, but if you think about it, the first week is spent being angry and full of the DTs. The last week is spent making plans to celebrate your release with your friends, probably at some trendy bar. So what you really have is two weeks in the middle to pretend you care and to try to get laid. We all know this is true. We watched the Sandra Bullock movie. (I am, of course, talking about the movie *28 Days,* not *Miss Congeniality 2,* which drove people to drink to escape the reality of having paid ten dollars to see that piece of crap.) Screwing around in rehab is why ugly people are the only ones who ever get cured of alcoholism. The good-looking people are having too much fun. The good news is, though, after a few years of being an alcoholic, you get fat and lose your teeth, and once you turn into an ugly person, you can get cured too.

Symbolic Rocks/Closing Ceremonies

Rehabbers use symbols like they used to use Jack Daniel's—and like the amount of Jack they used to use, it's enough to make the average person vomit. When you leave rehab they give you a rock, coin, or marble to take with you and carry around every day to remember your rehab stint in the real world. You'd think the $20,000 hit to your checking account or the stress-induced patch of gray hair would be enough of a gentle reminder. Instead of giving you a rock, they should give you something practical, like a T-shirt that says, "I spent twenty-eight days in hell and all I got was a lousy fucking pebble."

Symbolic rocks are really a reminder to never go to rehab again. The rocks are also really good for throwing at people who offer you heroin, pussy, cake, or whatever you're addicted to when you get out. They bless the rocks before they give them to you to make them more special than the ones that break your lawnmower. Since you make a lot of enemies in rehab, the blessing is about as heartfelt as when a stranger says, "Bless you," on the subway when you sneeze.

Sometimes the rocks say things like "Healing" or "Peace" on them. Yeah, that's going to keep you from relapsing. I want to do meth, but the little stone in my pocket says "Joy." I better not. If they really wanted to keep people from relapsing, they would give their sponsor a rock—a big heavy rock they could hit the addict in the head with every time he tried to do drugs. Think about it: That's a win-win situation. The drug addict still gets the blackout and time away from reality he wants, and society doesn't have to deal with another druggie in its midst. You could even write inspirational words right on the rock that the sponsor could say as they hit him—"Dumb Fuck" or "Nigga, Please." Let's face it, it's better to stone a guy half to death than coddle him and let him do drugs all the way to death. If we did this in the seventies, we'd still have Jim Morrison and Jimi Hendrix.

Acknowledgments

This book would only be an ache in my left nut if the following people hadn't helped make it happen: my hot 'n' tasty manager, Maggie Houlehan; the gruff but lovable J. P. Williams and everyone at Parallel Entertainment; Peter McGuigan; Nick Nuciforo, Sonya Rosenfeld, Martin Lesak, and everyone at CAA; Bob "Hottest Jew Ever" Bernstein; Joe Bartnick and Scott Dunn; Mike Smardak and everyone at Outback Concerts; Geof Wills and everyone at Live Nation; Yvette Shearer; Gaby the "Jew"ler on Forty-seventh Street in Manhattan; Andy Paige;

and, last but not least, Mauro DiPreta and Nancy Miller, the editors of my dreams.

A special thanks to Howard Stern and Don Rickles, the two funniest men who ever lived. I appreciate you inspiring me every single day.

Kisses to my honey bear, Jimmy, who gave me hugs through all the rough spots. I love you, baby!

And for their undying patience and support, my sister and brother, Nancy and Len, whom I look up to and admire. I love you both and want to be like you when I grow up!